POETRY REV

SUMMER 1997 VOLUME 8
EDITOR PETER FORBES
PRODUCTION STEPHEN TROUSSÉ
SUBSCRIPTIONS AND ADVERTISING SOPHIE JEPSON

CONTENTS

The Hoax Issue

ages 3 – 22

Peter Forbes on hoaxing; Gwyneth Lewis on forgery (6); The Sonnet History: John Whitworth on McGonagall (9); David Wheatley on Ern Malley (10); poem by "Stan Sheamey" (12); John Whitworth on plagiarism (13); poem by Glyn Maxwell (14); Tom Shapcott on Gwen Harwood (16); Jo Shapcott on W. D. Snodgrass (19); Adam Thorpe on Pessoa (21)

Poems

23 – 32

by George Szirtes, James Sutherland-Smith (24), Sarah Corbett, Wayne Burrows (25), Jayanta Mahapatra (26), Ruth Padel (27)

Interview

28 – 33

Mark Doty interviewed by Carole Satyamurti; poem by Mark Doty (31)

Poems

34 – 41

by Harry Clifton, John Mole (35), David Hart (36), Elizabeth Garrett, Atar Hadari (37), Simon Rae, Dorothy Nimmo (38), Michael Henry (39), Fred D'Aguiar (40), Matthew Sweeney, Matthew Hollis (41)

The Review Pages

42 – 54

Hermione Lee on *The School Bag*; Ian Sansom on Don Paterson (44); Philip Gross on Andrew Motion (46); Gillian Allnutt on Elaine Feinstein (47); poem by Elaine Feinstein (48)

The Classic Poem

49

Ruth Pitter's 'In the Open' chosen by Jenny Joseph

Reviews

50 – 55

Sean O'Brien on John Fuller: John Burnside on Geoffrey Hill (51), Jane Holland on Sappho (53), Ruth Padel on *The Odyssey* (54); Steve Ellis on Dante (55)

Poems

56 – 63

by John Goodby, Martyn Crucefix, Edwin Morgan (57), Greta Stoddart (58), David Wheatley (59), Paul Farley (60), Anthony Thwaite (61), Michael Longley, Martin Reed (62), Sinéad Morrissey (63)

Reviews

64 – 69

Harry Clifton on Auden; Lawrence Sail on Enzensberger (66), Dennis O'Driscoll on Dutch poetry (68); two poems by Anton Korweg (69)

New Poets '97

70 – 71

Poems by Gee Williams

Reviews

72 – 88

Michael Donaghy on the New Formalism; Helen Dunmore on Thomas Lynch (74); Maggie O'Farrell on James Harpur (75); Ian McMillan on first collections (76); Sheenagh Pugh on Iain Crichton Smith (78); Andrew Zawacki on David Hartnett and Jamie McKendrick (79); James Keery on Dick Davis and Iain Bamforth (80); 'Calling Ships at Sea' by Jenny Joseph (83); Tim Kendall on the Norton Anthology (84); William Scammell on Samuel Beckett (86); poem by David Moorcroft (87); Stephen Burt on Tony Harrison (88)

Appreciations

89 – 91

Adrian Mitchell on Allen Ginsberg; Anne Stevenson on Tom Rawling (90)

Poem by Ivy Garlitz (92)

Endstops

94 – 96

News & Comment, Competition, Letters

POETRY REVIEW
SUBSCRIPTIONS
Four issues including postage:

UK individuals £23
Overseas individuals £31
(all overseas delivery is by airmail)
USA individuals $56

Libraries, schools and institutions:
UK £30
Overseas £37
USA $66

Single issue £5.95 + 50p p&p (UK)

Sterling and US dollar payments only. Eurocheques, Visa and Mastercard payments are acceptable.

Bookshop distribution:
Password Books
Telephone 0161 953 4009

Design by Philip Lewis
Cover by Stephen Troussé

Typeset by Poetry Review.

Printed by Warwick Printing Co Ltd at Theatre Street, Warwick CV34 4DR and at 112 Bermondsey Street, London SE1 3TX
Telephone 0171 378 1579

POETRY REVIEW is the magazine of the Poetry Society. It is published quarterly and issued free to members of the Poetry Society. Poetry Review considers submissions from non-members and members alike. To ensure reply submissions must be accompanied by an SAE or adequate International Reply coupons: Poetry Review accepts no responsibility for contributions that are not reply paid.

Founded 24 February 1909
Charity Commissioners No: 303334
© 1997

EDITORIAL AND BUSINESS ADDRESS:
22 BETTERTON STREET, LONDON WC2H 9BU

telephone **0171 240 4810**
fax **0171 240 4818**
email **poetrysoc@dial.pipex.com**
website **http://www.poetrysoc.com**

THE POETRY SOCIETY

ISBN 1 900771 05 5
ISSN 0032 2156

Funded by THE ARTS COUNCIL OF ENGLAND

THE HOAX ENGINE

by Peter Forbes

SUDDENLY HOAXING HAS become a crucial sign and symptom of our society. Or rather, I should say, principally of the cultural laboratory of the Western world that is America. A recent issue of the *Boston Review*[1] refers in its editorial to "the emerging field of hoaxology: the study of deception, both deceivers, and dupes, particularly in contemporary cultural production". The issue contains a masterly analysis by Marjorie Perloff of the latest example from the poetry unit of contemporary cultural production: the spoof Hiroshima poet, Araki Yasusada, who took in the editors of *American Poetry Review*, *Grand Street*, and our very own *Stand* last year, only to be revealed as a hoax perpetrated by a white American academic, Kent Johnson, from Highland Community College, Freeport, Illinois.

Araki Yasusada was supposed to have been born in 1907 in Kyoto, moved to Hiroshima in 1921, and died in 1972 after a long struggle with cancer. "He has been a postman since 1927, and delivers the mail", says his biographical note. His notebooks were "discovered" in 1980 and formed the basis of a major feature in *American Poetry Review*[2].

Hoaxing, the use of alter egos and multiple personas have been an aspect of poetry for centuries but there are obvious reasons why it should be becoming an epidemic now. The modern world is driven by expectation, and if there is no natural occupant for a niche the pressure to invent becomes intense. And the temptation to subvert even stronger.

The classic hoax of recent years occurred in cultural studies of physics: Sokal's Hoax was so obviously the prototype of the Hiroshima hoax, it is worth looking at first. In contemporary American academic culture, physics and poetry are equally items of "cultural production" and subject to the same pressures and critical climate.

Alan Sokal is a New York based physicist who had become irritated by the decline in standards of academic rigour in the USA, especially in postmodernist appropriations of science. He published in the journal *Social Text* a hoax paper called 'Transgressing the Boundaries: Toward a Transformative Hermeneutics of Quantum Gravity'[3], which pressed as many fashionable

buttons as possible and was salted with scientific howlers and non-sequiturs.

Sokal gave the editors what they wanted to hear and they fell for it. He used many buzz words but the keynote repeated endlessly was "non-linear", a word that non-scientists don't understand but which, in postmodernist circles, has come to have an enormous plus value. Both Sokal and the Hiroshima Hoaxer told their audience what they wanted to hear in such an over-amplified manner the dissonance of error and absurdity was simply swamped.

What has all these got to do with the cultural product we still call poetry? Poetry has its plus words too, and the Yasusada Hoax mimicked Sokal's Hoax quite closely:

> The pi of Euclid and the G of Newton, formerly thought to be constant and universal, are now perceived in their ineluctable historicity.
>
> (Sokal)

> It does appear to us that these pieces [undated haiku] unmistakably bear the stamp of the famous poet, and Holocaust survivor, Paul Celan... It is known, from Ogiwara Seisensui's writing, that his work was read by the Layered Clouds group [pre-WWII] and critically discussed by them.
>
> (Yasusada's translators)

"Unmistakably", "ineluctable" – this is argument by hectoring, the reader being reminded by them that to dissent from party line concepts of added value is inconceivable, though in fact both statements are demonstrably false – pi cannot have a history; it is not a constant of the physical world but a property of mathematical relations; Yasuda couldn't have been influenced by Celan in the 'thirties because Celan wasn't published until 1952 and then only in German.

Both Sokal and the Hiroshima Hoaxer peppered their work with such give-aways, deliberately inviting discovery. Sokal refers to complex number theory as a "new and still quite speculative branch of mathematical physics" when it's actually something you do in 6th form maths. Yasusada is described as translating "with accuracy from six languages: French, English, Canadian, Australian, Zelandish, and Korean". A Yasusada poem of 1925 included the word "scubadivers" (invented in the 'forties). There was even a clue to the hoaxer's identity: the name of a friend of Johnson's – Howard McCord – was dropped into a list of American poets Yasusada was supposed to have been reading in 1967 (Snyder, Creeley, Ferlinghetti, etc).

The poems were received enthusiastically by many. The best reaction quoted by Perloff is Language poet Ron Silliman's. Here is the authentic voice of wrong-headed poetry appreciation, a man in thrall to what Perloff calls "a blinding preoccupation with writers' socio-cultural positions":

> There's an elevation of tone in these poems that reminds me more of Michael Palmer than Spicer [Jack Spicer, Yasusada's supposed great American influence], perhaps because the translators are all Hiroshima poets... These works kept me up last night and probably will again for another night or three. I recommend them highly.

The cluster of ideas which made the hoax possible include the following tenets:

1) The writer does not construct his poem – the culture writes the author (Foucault).

2) Where a poem comes from in the matrix of class, gender, economic power is more important than the textual meaning – positioning and empowerment are all.

3) Word like open, Eastern, decentred have added value; closed, Western, hegemonic negative value.

These criteria are highly congruent with the criteria for a postmodernist science: 1) science is culturally and historically conditioned, eg the indeterministic physics of the 'twenties followed the collapse of European hegemony in WWI; 2) science is a linguistic construct and language is self-referential, reflexive, unreliable, hence there is no reliable knowledge of the external world; 3) science is sexed, ie male-dominated, and politically oppressive; 4) vaguely metaphoric connections between such disciplines as psychoanalysis, topology, quantum mechanics, morphology, etc, can, if repeated often enough, constitute a synthetic framework of

revealed truth. Indeed the criteria for science and poetry alike are variants of the master set of rules for postmodernist cultural production – old-style production: patriarchal, authoritarian, deterministic, and as charismatic as John Major's underpants; new style postmodernist production: radically decentred, non-linear, changes the baby's nappies.

The fact that hoaxes which exploit these rules are so successful suggests that there is a strong element of willing into being behind the phenomenon. In fact, not only did the duped editors read into the work what they wanted to see, the rules themselves have been willed into being in the teeth of all the evidence against them.

* * * *

The prevalence of hoaxing in America has a curious wry inverted image in Britain: the collapse of the traditional ritual of hoaxing on April 1st. Mark Lawson has pointed out in the *Guardian*[4] that this year's newspaper hoaxes were so feeble and few as to suggest that April 1st is another moribund institution alongside the monarchy and the Tory Party. The April Fool requires that most of the time what the newspapers print is serious, however inaccurate or biased. This, together with the notorious assumption of the automatic authority of print, enables obvious nonsense to masquerade as truth for a paragraph or two at least. Lawson says: "The complication now is that stories which are ridiculous or exaggerated or untrue are now a staple of the media". In the land where, according to Will Self, Chris Morris is God (and Cake was *the* hoax of the year) what chance does an ordinary April Fool have? (Ah, take me back to San Seriffe!). Lawson goes on: "The cruel truth is that we have lost the right to choose when we want to be disbelieved".

There is another related reason that the April Fool's time is up – it is traditional, ie it has no logo, no red noses, no bucket shop promoting it – it is just there, like kid's street games and nursery rhymes, something we pass on unofficially. This isn't good enough for the age of cultural production. No logo and you're dead. The Police aren't just Police any more, they're Crimestoppers with a hotline. Even the Queen has a website, for God's sake. April 1st could still make it if it acquired those accoutrements. Write a mission statement. Put in a lottery bid. Line up some star endorsements. Start planning for 2000 NOW!

But lest we get too gloomy, this issue was conceived because hoaxes are both fun and instructive. Fake poets may sometimes be needed because real ones have left a gap. Britain today has two of the finest: E. J. Thribb and Jason Strugnell.

Private Eye's long-standing Poet in Residence, Eric Jarvis Thribb (perpetually 17 years old), has been the characteristic elegist of our era. All of the dead great and good have been commemorated by him in the only verse form truly appropriate to our times, a floundering free verse that gasps to find anything appropriate to say. The poems ironize the achievements of the famous by pointing out the contradictions inherent in their role.

Thribb also invented the great Everywoman persona, Keith's Mum, to add her vox pop commentary – a sobering counterpoint to Thribb's insouciantly youthful irreverence. By combining an old and a young voice in this way, Thribb effortlessly predated the rise of anti-ageism, anti-sexism and anti-classism.

Thribb's name is in itself a poem of course: E. J. being reminiscent of Auden's W. H. but also invoking in its consonantal music the E. L. of Wisty, Peter Cook's phenomenally boring character who was clearly one of Thribb's formative influences. Then of course the name Thribb is the Pooter *de nos jours*, a name of "diminished expectations", a Larkinian bicycle-clip of a name.

Illustration by BIFF

Jason Strugnell is a typical product of the provincial and suburban poetry workshops that flourished from the 'seventies on. Judging by the internal evidence of 'Sonnet v' Strugnell was born around 1938. His stamping ground is the South London of Tulse Hill and Norwood. By temperament Strugnell is somewhat sluggish, his verse, in the words of his lovingly imitated Shakespeare, "far from variation or quick change". But it is this very dullness that enabled him to bring the art of bathos to a new peak. Strugnell's heroically unheroic stance made him the only poet able to take on the challenge of Shakespeare's Sonnets and make something effortlessly late 20th century of them. Not even Eliot could bring bathos to the point of "I need a woman, honest and sincere, / Who'll come across on half a pint of beer". And the characteristic pleasures of the age have never been more truly sung

than in 'Sonnet v': "And yet I still have my guitar to strum / And books to read and some fantastic grass / that Tony got me" (Tony of course is a good friend of E. J. Thribb's Keith).

And sometimes a hoax hoaxes the hoaxer. The poetry of Ern Malley was summoned into being to protest at certain tendencies in Modernist poetry (see p10). But its satire was too good and was hence taken as the real thing. For if Ern Malley was a fraud ("In the twenty fifth year of my age") so were Dylan Thomas, George Barker ("You have hawked in your throat and spat / Outrage at velocipedes of thriftless / Mechanical men..."), Auden ("Rise from the wrist, o kestrel / Mind, to a clear expanse"), and the rest of the Modernist pantheon plundered by Malley. Malley's work is pastiche, full of grotesque lurches in register, bathetic absurdities and mock profundities. But what Modernist poem isn't? That litany constitutes a definition of Modernism. Because they're fakes we should perhaps not regard the Ern Malley poems as Modernist, but in their subversion of the compact between between writer, words and the world they now seem quintessentially postmodern. Whatever, the poems are alive to this day and included in anthologies because in sitting down to write rubbish McAuley and Stewart effectively evaded the internal verse policeman who would have made them write dull conventional poems of the time. Let hoaxing thrive.

1. Marjorie Perloff, 'In Search of the Authentic Other', *Boston Review*, Vol 22 No 2, April-May 1997. This can be accessed on the web at http://www.polisci.mit.edu/BostonReview/
2. 'Doubled Flowering: From the Notebooks of Araki Yasusada', translated by Tosa Motokiyu, Okura Kyojin, and Ojiu Norinaga, *American Poetry Review*, July/August 1996, pp23–26.
3. Alan Sokal, 'Transgressing the Boundaries: Toward a Transformative Hermeneutics of Quantum Gravity', *Social Text*, Summer 1996, pp217–252.
4. Mark Lawson, 'April Fool? It's a joke', *The Guardian*, 3 April 1997.

With thanks to Stephen Burt for alerting me to the Hiroshima Hoax.

Three Faces of Forgery

GWYNETH LEWIS FLIRTS WITH SOME DANGEROUS CHARMERS

EVERYBODY LOVES A forger. Like certain men (whom your mother takes against) – you know you shouldn't but they just seem so much more interesting than the more genuine articles on offer. They appeal to the rebel in all of us, the part that cheers at anybody who gets one over on the establishment, any kind of expert who takes himself seriously. We like to know how the real thing can be substituted by an object or work which has no intrinsic value but the appearance of value. The forger confirms our sneaking suspicion that art is a trick, that any of us could produce what could be taken by gullible critics as a masterpiece, if only we had the chutzpah and the sheer cleverness to bring it off.

In the late 'eighties I spent a number of years thinking about forgery as a cultural phenomenon. By mistake, I ended up writing a doctorate in Oxford on the subject. Yes, it had more popular appeal as a subject than the use of periphrasis in Dickens but I should, perhaps, have been doing other, better, things with my life. It's easy to range up behind a rogue who's bucked the system; we enjoy vicariously the perverse heroism of being maligned, misunderstood or simply not given credit for work well done although it might involve laughing all the way to the bank. As I see it now, this question of credit is a central one in the work of these forgers, and offers very important clues to the rest of us why you should, artistically speaking, after playing around a bit, go for men your mother can at least talk to over a cup of tea and some cake.

There are three degrees of forgery. The first is blatant. You make a Mexican primitive sculpture of a squatting god and flog it in an auction house as a Mayan relic. The work fetches such a high price that you think you must now be a great artist, so you blab, tell the world it was really you and then can't understand why everybody turns away in disgust and the possibility of jail is mentioned.

The second degree of forgery is culturally determined. Eighteenth-century Britain (the subject of my thesis) was rich in these. People like Thomas Chatterton passing off his "medieval" Rowley poems and manuscripts (the parchment of which he'd "antiquated" by rubbing it on a window) partly because the market place for ancient texts was, at that time, much more rewarding than that for

nearly first-rate poetry by a young Bristolian without connections. Or James Macpherson, who "discovered" fragments of a Gaelic epic in the oral culture of the Highlands, which he published and launched as the Ossian poems, with their laments for a butchered people; they were a huge success, particularly in Germany. Or William Henry Ireland, a young man who "discovered" new Shakespearean texts, including the play *Vortigern*, showing that the Bard was really a Republican, a very controversial and politically charged position to take in the aftermath of the French Revolution.

Then there was my main man, Edward Williams, or Iolo Morganwg, a Welsh-speaking polymath, laudanum addict, radical Unitarian and poet. Iolo walked to London in the 1770s and worked there as a stonemason. He met Dr. Johnson in a bookshop and, according to Iolo, asked him politely which grammar of English would he recommend. "*Either of them* will do for you, *young man*", came the reply, whereupon Iolo bought all three of the books he was considering, although he couldn't afford them. Thus perhaps began a long story of cultural resentment which led to the extraordinary druidic forgeries which became his main lifetime achievement. Iolo's first collection of English-language verse, *Poems, Lyric and Pastoral*, was published in 1794. The book was a critical success in London but obviously left the poet disappointed with its reception. As Iolo became more radical in response to the events of the French Revolution it became increasingly dangerous for him to express his political and religious views openly in Britain. Indeed, he found it difficult to attract the literary patronage which was necessary for a comfortable life in London and his papers were searched by the authorities. His response to this was twofold. He returned to Wales and switched to writing mainly in Welsh, in an antiquarian idiom, so that his views would be invisible to the government. Using the pedagogic device of the bardic triad, Iolo pieced together an ambitious history of the Gorsedd of the Bards (literally, the "assembly" or "convocation" of the bards) on which the modern Eisteddfod pageantry is based. As he felt marginalized by his own society he envisaged an order of artists who were at the very centre of theirs.

It was as if Tony Blair had made the Martians High Court Judges. In Iolo's imaginary world (a kind of wish-list located in the past) poets were the guardians of ancient British literature, law and religion. Read as a whole, these writings represent a remarkable radical response to political events of the period. Had there been free speech at the time, these documents would not have been written.

What I discovered in my research was that the term "forgery" is not an absolute identifier of fabrication but, rather, a politically charged word which could be used to dismiss a kind of writing coming from the fringes of Britain that made some of the critics at the centre feel uncomfortable. I have a control in this experiment. When James Macpherson heard scraps of an ancient epic being recited in the Scottish Highlands he did what any mid-eighteenth-century editor would do: he wrote them down, tidied them up by adding sections of his own verse and published them as ancient poetry. This is exactly what Bishop Thomas Percy did in his famous collection of ballads, *Reliques of Ancient English Poetry*. Far from being reviled in London as a forger, as Macpherson was, Percy's work was well received by, among others, Dr. Johnson. He was a bishop and was patronised by the Earl of Northumberland's family. He was not an outsider, and did not represent a claim for the excellence of the Celtic strand of British poetry. When is a forger not a forger? When he's a jolly good editor.

Like Iolo Morganwg, who was a radical Unitarian, Thomas Chatterton, the "wondrous boy", held unorthodox religious beliefs which did not enhance his own reputation as a poet. Jacob Bryant, one of the most vociferous supporters of the authenticity of the Rowley poems, was frankly insulting about the *African Eclogues* which Chatterton published under his own name. He also disliked this work because they were heavily influenced by the Ossian poems, with their sonorous invocations of warriors of the past, their mood of rolling doom and of lost glory. Moreover, Chatterton's claims for the importance of Bristol's culture and history and for the Saxon/Ossianic element in English poetry made him a highly contentious figure, although he was never as politically suspect as William Ireland or Iolo Morganwg.

The reason why these "culturally determined" forgers are worth bothering with in the long run is that they were all interesting avant-garde writers who explored the early poetry of the British Isles as a modern idiom. Some of this resulted in quasi anti-quarian dottiness, but much of the writing is of lasting value and interest, mining a poetic vein which had already been explored successfully in English by Thomas Gray in 'The Bard', which started gloriously: "Ruine seize thee, ruthless King! / Confusion on thy banners wait!". The Ossian poetry, read in moderation, is striking and has a melancholy Old Testament feel to it which is genuinely moving. For example:

> By the side of a rock on the hill, beneath the aged trees, old Ossian sat on the moss; the last of the race of Fingal. Sightless are his aged eyes, his beard is waving in the wind. Dull through the leafless trees he heard the voice of the north. Sorrow revived in his soul: he began and lamented the dead.

Forgers from the first category I described are usually failed artists who hitch a ride on the back of their superiors in art. Their style is rarely convincing for more than a generation and is always only an imitation of another's. For example, it's clear to everyone who's spent any time looking at art that Van Meegeren's Vermeer, *Christ and the Disciples at Emmaus*, is a 1930s copy. But this was very difficult for contemporaries to see. The work of the forgers of the second degree has a lasting life, despite politically motivated attempts to dismiss it as the product of mischief-makers.

Indeed, the Iolo Morganwg forgeries can be seen as an extension of the legitimate myth-manufacturing which goes on in the creation of any national entity and I've no doubt that with the forthcoming referendum on Devolution his stock will again be high in Wales, especially if the measure is passed.

But even these second-order forgers, however, well-intentioned and appealing, are not entirely to be admired in the canons of literature, as they have brought, albeit unintentionally, the cause of poetry into disrepute. The very act of "smuggling" native British poetry into the literary mainstream on the back of a beefed-up antiquity compromised the strength of that important push towards the centre. Thomas Gray's 'The Bard' was a hit without any attempt to give a false pedigree to the material (although it has to be said that the myth on which the poem is based is itself of doubtful provenance, but this is par for the course with Celtic myths).

Forgers always get caught out. Because they use methods which don't entirely stand up to scrutiny, they always hand their opponents the most damaging weapons against themselves. No wonder the

Chatterton we remember is the suicide in his despair, artistically draped across a sofa.

Although poets like Macpherson, Chatterton and Iolo were at the forefront of a revival of native British poetry in London, the very mechanisms which they chose to assault the citadel meant that their success could only be partial. Part of the problem was that they were all writing in order to prove a theory – that the Scottish oral tradition was heroic, along classical lines, that the ancient Welsh bards were civilised and not mere butchers of virgins, that Bristol could produce refined poetry in medieval times. Had they been part of a government machine, these men would have been propagandists. They predated their literary cheques, giving their present preoccupations a false historical pedigree. Just because they were on the opposing, losing side doesn't mean that their work wasn't just as compromised by the need to prove a pre-ordained point as that of those artists who subscribed to Socialist Realism. A forger always has a point to make. This never makes great poetry, which is always discovered as the writer surfs through metre, never really knowing at the beginning where the hell he or she is going.

The situation isn't helped by the fact that the axe which these forgers have to grind usually has to do with one branch of literature being neglected. Read too much Ossian and you start to want to butcher the bards yourself. William Henry Ireland began forging because he wanted to prove his own value to his father, Samuel, who was besotted with all things Shakespearean. Once he had furnished the bard-obsessed father with a number of legal documents, William had to go one better and write a whole play which received a humiliating première.

The real pathos of the story lies, however, in Samuel Ireland's refusal to believe that the documents were fakes, even after his son published a full confession. He died protesting their authenticity. This adherence to fantasy, and in such public manner, suggests some of the deeper psychological mechanisms at work in the activity of forgery – the heartbreaking desire to please, the drive for recognition at whatever cost to the truth, and the terrible disappointments caused to others when the illusion crumbles. Forgers are always at least as concerned with the effect their work has on others as with its quality, which is why, perhaps, they're never free enough as artists to do creative work of the first rank which will outlast the novelty of their cases.

Which brings me to the third degree of forgery.

W.H. Auden put his finger on the temptation of forgery when he defined it as a poem which he should not have written. On the face of it, this seems an inadequate description of forgery because it doesn't take into account the cultural complexities outlined above. However, he cuts to the heart of the impulse and puts his finger on a basic dishonesty which can inform even work which we write in a modern idiom and under our own names.

I struggle all the time not to write forgeries. These are the poems which I would like to write, which would make me feel good, flattered and which, more importantly, I think would make me look good in others' eyes. In my case these might include grievance poems (towards men, the world in general and, in particular, lamenting the loss of a Celtic Golden Age). This is not to say that these aren't perfectly valid subjects for poems, but they're not for me. They bring out that whiney, I've-been-wronged tone of voice and are always embarrassing to read afterwards because I haven't actually mentioned what a cow I was or how there never was a Golden Age anyway or, even more importantly, how I might have contributed to its ending.

The new climate of political correctness poses a significant temptation to forgery by poets. Twm Morys, a Welsh-language poet of delightful inventiveness, recounts a hilarious story of a recent visit to America. In a symposium, having read a poem in which he imagined himself as a bird talking to a woman (a very old convention in Welsh poetry) he was astonished to be asked by a member of the audience what gave him the right to think he knew how a bird felt. This is dangerous nonsense; as well as being the most soul-destroying kind of literalism, it attacks the great and substantial virtues of the imagination which, when exercised properly, make things more real rather than less so.

Forged poetry is often in itself bland because the premise upon which it's written is so outrageous that the perpetrator tiptoes around hoping you won't notice the real issue, which is its semi-authenticity. Real poetry – and by that I mean poetry that I and only I should write – is not as innocuous. It tells me what I need but often don't want to know. With the help of rhyme and metre it guides me safely down into the unconscious and allows me to approach subjects and events which, without the protection of beauty, would be too painful to see. A forger is always far too easy to like (because he's arranged it that way). But you should listen to your mother. In the long run, he always lets you down.

THE SONNET HISTORY

JOHN WHITWORTH
PERFORMING POET

I sing a man born in 1830 and dead
A year before the "good and charitable Sovereign" to whom
    he wrote his
Famous Jubilee Ode. I sing a man said
To be "the greatest bad poet of his age" – the quote is

From *Punch*, not-notably-poetic organ of the Philistines.
Many a poet (Yeats for instance) is an unconscious
    comedian,
And our man's works mature like the finest wines.
For I sing William McGonagall, "Poet and Tragedian",

Whose influence on English, and Scottish, Poetry will
    never ever fade,
Who performed, "in a strong voice with great enthusiasm" ,
    causing streets to be crowded "from head to foot",
    and multitudes to weep all,
Who was a poor man living for his art, a weaver by trade,
Like bully Bottom, another poet of the people.

So, in "stentorian voices as loud as we can bawl", let's
    give three hearty cheers
For one of our bardic persuasion whose works have been
    continuously in print for over a hundred years!

Splitting the Infinitive: Ern Malley

DAVID WHEATLEY ON THE POETIC HOAX OF THE CENTURY

IN 1939 FLANN O'Brien published a comic novel, *At Swim-Two-Birds*, whose hero is an unexceptional young man in every way but one: he was "born at the age of twenty-five". Four years later, on the other side of the world, another young man pulled off an even more audacious stunt: Ern Malley, described by the poet and editor Max Harris as "one of the most remarkable and important poetic figures of this country" died at the same age without ever having been born. His *oeuvre* amounted to a mere sixteen poems, which he had grouped under the mysterious title *The Darkening Ecliptic*. Unpublished in his lifetime, the poems were discovered after his death by his sister Ethel as she went through his papers in the Melbourne suburb where he worked as an insurance salesman. Although not a literary person herself, she felt she ought to do something about them and sent them to *Angry Penguins*, the brash new magazine edited by the Adelaide poet Max Harris. Ern had died of Graves' disease, Ethel informed Harris, a disease one of whose symptoms is bulging eyes. Not even Graves' disease could have made Harris's eyes bulge any wider than they did when he turned from Ethel's witless covering letter to the first of Ern's poems, 'Dürer: Innsbruck, 1495'. It was a revelation. As he read on, his excitement only increased. Here at last was the radical modernist which stuffy colonial Australia had been waiting for, a poet who knew his Villon and his Mallarmé; someone who had modernized himself, as Pound said of Eliot, on his own – only to die, unknown to his countrymen, at twenty-five. Plans were immediately set in train for a commemorative issue of *Angry Penguins*. Soon Ern Malley would be famous, and Australian writing dragged reluctantly into the modernist age.

It was not to be. "I had read in books that art is not easy / But no one warned that the mind repeats / In its ignorance the vision of others", Malley had written in 'Dürer: Innsbruck, 1495'. Little did Harris suspect in his ignorance exactly whose vision he was about to reproduce in the pages of *Angry Penguins*. The whole thing was a hoax, concocted in a single afternoon by Corporal Harold Stewart and Lieutenant James McAuley of the Directorate of Research and Civil Affairs, a wartime think-tank designed to keep intellectuals such as Stewart and McAuley out of mischief. Why did they do it? As Michael Heyward shows in the definitive book *The Ern Malley Affair**, Australian poetry at the time was sharply divided into different camps and schools. Jealousies and antagonisms ran deep. A. D. Hope, then as now a grey eminence of Australian poetry, referred disparagingly to the contemporary poets "of whom I know so little and by whom for the most part I am profoundly bored or irritated". The colonial view that a writer had to publish in London to be taken seriously was still widespread. In an effort to counter this, the Jindyworobak movement campaigned to return Australian poetry to its native inheritance. Its founder, Rex Ingamells, had hard words for the cultural cringe which bedevilled Australian life, writing in 1942: "We, the Australian people, are the hollowest of shams, the most pitiful pretentiousness that the tragic spark of life has contrived; the most ashen gutter the brief candle of spiritual existence has given to the dreams of civilisation". Although anti-colonial, the Jindyworobaks were also opposed to foreign influences; these were strictly Max Harris's department. Ridiculing the work of Ingamells and his associates as the "Jabberwocky" school, Harris had founded *Angry Penguins* to give a platform to his cosmopolitan tastes, which ran to Rimbaud, Seferis, Baudelaire and Henry Miller and heavy doses of the English Apocalypse. It was the most outlandish magazine Australian poetry had ever seen.

McAuley and Stewart looked on in horror, and decided that enough was enough. Having written the Malley poems, they invented his Edna Everage-like sister Ethel as a cover, and put the lot in the post. Harris's ecstatic response was just what they wanted: with the fusewire safely lit, all they had to do was wait for the petard to hoist. *Angry Penguins* duly appeared, and rumours began to circulate almost immediately. "Ern Malley, the great poet or the greatest hoax?" screamed the front page of *Fact*, a Sydney daily not usually noted for its interest in

*Michael Heyward, *The Ern Malley Affair*, Faber, 1993

the fine arts. Eventually Stewart and McAuley came clean. They had perpetrated the hoax to expose the low critical standards of editors like Harris, responsible for "the gradual decay of meaning and craftsmanship in poetry"; the issues at stake, they claimed, were no laughing matter. What had seemed like a piece of innocent high-jinks began to take on a more serious air, not that the philistine readers of *Fact* would have cared very much. The comedy turned even sourer three months later when Harris suddenly found Malley's work at the centre of an obscenity trial. The attempts by the Australian press to make sense of it had been bad enough, but not even they could match the absurdity of Detective Vogelsang for the prosecution. "I think it unusual for the sexual parts to be referred to in poetry", he asseverated. The judge agreed and fined Harris £5. It was a crushing blow to Harris's morale. *Angry Penguins* tried to carry on, but soon stopped publishing. Although he returned to editing, the Malley stigma would cling to him all his life.

What of the poems themselves: were they really "devoid of literary merit", as McAuley and Stewart declared in their press release after being rumbled? The strange thing to a contemporary reader is that, no they weren't. Could the hoaxers have fooled themselves and produced real poetry despite their stated intentions? Or as Stephen Dedalus asks in James Joyce's *A Portrait of the Artist as a Young Man*: if a man hacking at a block of wood accidentally produces a likeness of a cow, is the image a work of art? To judge from the defence of Malley which he launched, Harris thought so. He continued to praise the poems, published them as a separate volume and answered his gleeful critics with the words "I still believe in Ern Malley". He had every reason to: Dadaist moments aside, *The Darkening Ecliptic* is a thoughtful piece of writing whose philosophical themes and reflections on writing and language are not unlike late W. S. Graham.

Illustration by BIFF

The barminess is offset by humour ("Knowst not, my Lucia, that he / Who has caparisoned a nun dies / With his twankydillo at the ready?"), and some of the images are remarkable ("the black swan of trespass on alien waters"). As here, many passages read like veiled comments on their fabricated origins: "If this be the norm / Of our serious frolic / There's no remorse", he tells us after a leg-pullingly arcane passage of 'Sonnets for the Novachord'; in 'Culture as Exhibit' he hints that "There is a meaning for the circumspect". 'Egyptian Register' ends with Ern invoking "the mausoleum of my incestuous / And self-fructifying death" before slipping away in the last poem, 'Petit Testament', with the words: "I have split the infinitive. Beyond is anything". Max Harris was not alone in admiring the poems: in England Herbert Read came to their defence, while in America a youthful John Ashbery was impressed, and crestfallen to learn that no new Malley poems would be appearing.

So who was fooling whom? The subsequent career of at least one of the pranksters, Harold Stewart, is a cautionary example of how a hoax can – appropriate word – boomerang. As Malley continued to grow in fame, Stewart came to hate the way in which this youthful *jeu d'esprit* had outshone the rest of his work: in John Tranter and Philip Mead's *Penguin Book of Modern Australian Poetry* (1991), for instance, Stewart's "own" work is nowhere to be seen but *The Darkening Ecliptic* is reprinted in its entirety. Keen to get away, Stewart moved to Japan in 1966, where he dedicated himself to a quiet life of haiku-writing until his recent death. McAuley's way of distancing himself from Malley was a conservative spiral away from all things modernist, calling for a return to eighteenth-century poetic values and helping to found a right-wing Catholic political party. It was not until the late 'sixties that Australia witnessed anything like a modernist (or by this stage, postmodernist) movement in poetry again.

If the Malley affair had a demoralizing effect on experimentalism in Australia, it also set a precedent for a rich tradition of literary hoaxes which continues to this day. Finding it difficult as a young housewife to be taken seriously by the *Sydney Bulletin*, Gwen Harwood (1920-1995) invented several male personae who had no such problems — or at least not until "Walter Lehmann" was found to have spelt the words "So long Bulletin" and "Fuck all editors" acrostically in two of his sonnets (see p16). More recently hoaxes have erupted in Australian fiction: first the Demidenko affair, in which a prize-winning novel about the Ukrainian famine of the 'thirties, presented as the author's family history, was unmasked as the work of the distinctly un-Ukrainian Helen Darville and accused of serious plagiarism; and second the Radley affair, in which a prize-winning novel published by the teenager Paul Radley in 1980 was discovered sixteen years later to be by his uncle, a deception which Radley claimed left him deeply depressed and unable to hold down a job. If a lot more self-confident than it was fifty years ago, Australian poetry today is no less capable of bitter in-fighting than in Max Harris's time: perhaps a new Malley is being groomed as an antidote to the dangerous excesses of Les Murray, Peter Porter or Dorothy Hewett even as I write.

In his story "Pierre Menard, Author of Don Quixote" Jorge Luis Borges proposes a radical new theory of reading based on deliberately "erroneous attribution", inviting us to contemplate the *Imitatio Christi* as a work of Céline or Joyce. My candidates for reattribution in contemporary poetry would include *Zoom!* as written by R. S. Thomas, *The Mercian Hymns* by Sophie Hannah and *The Spirit Level* by Iain Sinclair. What surer way to overturn the age-old cultural imperialism of the canonical author? Poems could be given free transfers, like footballers since the Bosman ruling, from one author to another. Poetry prizes could be replaced by lotteries in which the winning ticket would qualify the holder for authorship of a masterpiece of his or her choice. There is hardly a corner of the poetry world that the spirit of Ern could not infiltrate: editorials, reviews, the page you are currently reading... Look at that byline again: David who? Try to picture the letter that came with this article: "Dear Peter Forbes, when I was going through my brother's papers after his death, I found an essay on Ern Malley he had written..."

David Wheatley recently co-edited an Australian special issue of *Metre* magazine. He has also published under various pseudonyms.

STAN SHEAMAY
BLACK PASTORAL

Gathered grass of his goat's beard
Evocative in the hog-strewn days of summer;
And his eyes blue and innocent, the old lecher.

Stagnant beneath his beamed brows
The brackish waters of a stunted past . . .
His son differs from him as sullen from sunlight.

The two tramped over cracked fields,
The sun's gauze laughing in their wake;
And the old man whistled for rain;

As his right foot crushed a rotting rook.

[MICHAEL SHEARER, STANLEY J. THOMAS AND GERDA MAYER]

GERDA MAYER WRITES:

No poem so meaningless but will find an editor or two to give it houseroom. We three were going by car to Thaxted, when the radiator overheated, which made the journey a rather slow one. In order to pass the time, each of us took it in turn to supply a line of verse. By the time we arrived, we had a complete poem, wholly gibberish of course, but I considered that it had a certain air. So I provided a title and an "author" made up from sections of our names. Places like *London Magazine* wisely refused it. However two cheerfully scruffy magazines of the time (?1972), *Bogg* and *Your Friendly Fascist* promptly published it, one even giving it pride of place.

Whose Lines Are They Anyway?

by John Whitworth

NEAL BOWERS

The Hunt For A Plagiarist

W W Norton, £12.95
ISBN 0 393 04007 0

LITERATURE IS GENERATED by the system. Individuals are not the authors of works of Literature. All Literature is made up of echoes of other Literature. Plagiarism is therefore impossible. At least, that's what Jacques Derrida, Deconstructionist Post-Structuralist, says and he is still the main man where Literature is taught

A computer can be programmed to write Elizabethan sonnets. I read this somewhere, though it didn't say whether the sonnets were any good. Actually I don't think you are *allowed* to say whether things are any good. Not if you're a Deconstructionist Post-Structuralist.

Bad poets borrow. Good poets steal. Marlowe stole from Spenser – stole great chunks. Shakespeare stole from North, Golding, Holinshed – not just "ideas" but words and phrases. Pope stole from Dryden. The best lines in *Four Quartets* are stolen.

Students writing essays for their B.A.s are not supposed to copy wholesale from published books and articles. This is still called plagiarism. The guilty student can theoretically fail an exam. But though I am told that the practice is widespread – exams are all takeaways now – the charge is almost never allowed to stick. A student is a customer, you see, and a failing student is a dissatisfied customer. Bowers has an example of this:

Henry Taylor's poems were appropriated by a graduate student for part of his doctoral thesis. When Taylor protested ... he found the student's thesis committee were more eager to avoid a messy academic situation than to hold the student accountable.

Quite!

Fifty years ago Hugh MacDiarmid stole (in the words of Gavin Ewart) "a piece of prose about a bird / and passed it off as his own poem". He also stole good bits from Thomas Mann. Rumbled, he said it was an accident and anyhow great poets could. Ezra Pound did.

Recently a boy stole an article from *The Economist* and published it as his own. He won £200 for himself and £300 for his school from *The Guardian*, though I think they had to give the money back. Rumbled, he said (doubtless shrugging) he had not thought *The Economist* was widely read.

The journo whose article was pilfered did his own shrugging. All journalism is plagiarising, he said, or words to that effect. He obviously felt his position was somehow ridiculous.

This feeling of ridiculousness descended on Neal Bowers when he found a David Sumner had stolen a Bowers poem in *Mankato Poetry Review*. In fact 'David Sumner' stole many poems, from Bowers (two poems *twenty* times), from Sharon Olds, Robert Gibb, Marcia Hurlow, Mark Strand...

Bowers spent time and money – he paid a lawyer – tracking the thief down. David Sumner (or Johns or Ahlstrom or Compton or Diane Compton) was David Jones, a failed poet and ex-primary school teacher who had lost his teacher's licence, and indeed gone to jail, for molesting seven-year-old girl pupils in his classroom.

And so Jones became a plagiarist. Did you know that the root meaning of Latin *plagiarius* is a kidnapper, a stealer-away of slaves and children? Odd.

Few of Bowers' male friends took the plagiarism

seriously (the guy's a nut – leave it alone). Women were more sympathetic. Bowers seems the sort of person women generally are more sympathetic to – you know, a bit earnest, or maybe that's just American.

Would I, for instance, care as much as this?

The poem was a bittersweet bloom I planted on my father's grave. The thief dug it up, pruned it to his liking, and damaged the roots in the process. He replanted it in the soil mounded over my father and pretended the loss was his.

I don't honestly think that I would. Would you, dear Reader? Has gender anything to do with it? Are women's poems more personal, as sentimental Kingsley Amis said?

Why did Jones do it? Not for money surely. There just wasn't *enough*. For the buzz of seeing his name (well, not his name exactly but a name he had used) in print? To make editors/poets look stupid? We have all had that urge I think.

Years ago an editor – Tim Longville of *Grossteste Review* it was; I haven't forgotten – rejected my verses, saying they all used the same trick and the trick belonged to Larkin anyway. Trick? Is poetry a trick? (He was talking about *your* poetry Whitworth. Shut up.) As I was saying, is a poet's verbal magic just conjuring, sleight of hand, deceit, lies, as Plato thought?

Craig Raine invented Martian poetry and other Martians followed. What were they doing? Parodying? Copying? Not exactly plagiarising surely?

Could anybody do it? No, I don't think so. The manner needs a certain amount of wit. Could you programme a computer to write Martian poetry? If you were a witty programmer, then I think you could. As an editor, Craig Raine was always wanting me to rewrite my poems (I did too). To make them better? To make them more Martian? Would that be the same thing?

Writers are supposed to find their "voice". That's what the books and courses say. But suppose the voice belongs to someone else? How can you know a thing like that? It's worse if you are writing *American* poetry, poetry that doesn't rhyme or scan; it so nakedly depends on that individual "voice". Jones made small changes (*à la* MacDiarmid) to the Bowers poems he stole. One editor said that some of these changes were improvements. That *really* got to Bowers, as it would to me.

When Gavin Ewart wrote 'The Larkin Automatic Car Wash' he said it wasn't a parody, more a kind of homage. Ewart also wrote Brownings, Strugnells, McGonagalls. When I asked him years ago about his twenty years of poetic silence, he said that all the poems he wrote in the 'forties came out as Betjemans. And before the war they were Audens. (Actually they were always authentic Ewarts.) There is a related problem which didn't trouble chameleon Ewart. Suppose the author you are parodying/plagiarising turns out to be yourself. What do you do then? Shut up? Is that what happened to Wordsworth? To Larkin? Does it ever happen to you?

I wrote a poem lately and it turned into a Sophie Hannah. I don't think she would agree, but that's the way it seemed. And it's the only grown-up poem I've written for a couple of years (except for the Sonnet History, that is).

All the rest – and my God the *facility* – belong to an alter ego, a ten-year-old girl called Phoebe Flood Phoebe Flood/Sophie Hannah? Am I changing my sex? (You should be so lucky, Whitworth.) Jeremy Reed told me his poems were dictated by a child with the face of Shelley. Was he having me on? The dreadful Derrida may be a charlatan but charlatans can be on to something. Read this book. It's short and interesting.

GLYN MAXWELL
THE STUFF OF COMEDY

You don't want to lose me
But you think I ought to go.
I'm the stuff of comedy
    If you must know.

I have no idea what's coming,
And it's sure to find me out.
I'm the stuff that comedy
    Can't do without.

There are many of us here
And we look and dress like you
When you dress like something comedy
    Requires you to.

You can ask us any questions now
Though when somebody does
We'll be giving answers comedy
    Demands of us.

Although to us they couldn't make
More sense, the rules we know
(By heart like you know sketches
    From an old live show)

To you they are what only gets us
Hurt or shamed or splattered.
It's vintage comedy to think rules
    Really mattered.

At dawn we joke we are in hell
Under a guttering star.
This joke becomes a classic when
    You see we are.

The others who were comedy
For years for being others
Have long been treated carefully as
    Half brothers,

But we march on forever with our
Big packs strapped tight,
Burdened in that blazing orphan-
    Making light

We thought was shining on *our* day.
It only made us blind
To you, in black, decades away,
    Corpsing behind,

And pointing it wherever you
See movement. Glad to say
What's comic turns up endlessly,
    Like DNA,

The difference being we comic turns
Can't see beyond our noses.
That's why we look so dumb on film
    In fighting poses.

We have no self-awareness, that's
A new advance in Man.
Can't think what we'd have done with it
    But you can.

For had we seen you, rest assured
Each would have glanced across
At nothing, having got the joke
    Alone of us,

And I myself would strip right off
And tear the rules to shreds,
And split my sides with laughter
    At the blockheads.

And be the one they always knew
Was vaguely out to tea.
Which technically you know as *tragi-*
    Comedy.

When only one knows where he is.
I'm one who thinks he does,
Whatever beams out of Atlantis
    Back at us.

I'm one who thinks that city knows
Some jokes you wouldn't get.
But that's what I call comedy.
    What isn't yet.

Like what will bring you into lines
Opaque as poetry
When seen far off through water like
    Atlantisians see.

Like us who you can't see for tears
When laughing makes you cry,
Like something's trying to show who's really
    Saying goodbye.

The Faces of Gwen Harwood

TOM SHAPCOTT ON A WORTHY SUCCESSOR TO ERN MALLEY

"THAT'S ME! THAT was a poem about me!" Old Mrs Foster came up full of delight and excitement to me and the little group of listeners after the lecture/reading by Vincent Buckley on the poet Gwen Harwood. The year was 1963. The place: Queensland University.

"Which poem?" I asked. Mrs Foster was Gwen Harwood's mum.

"Oh, the elegy, of course, the one about my death."

Mrs Foster had become an old cohort of mine. Some months before, in 1962, Mrs Foster had been a playful party in yet another of her daughter's literary games. She had relished that immensely, too. In that year Rodney Hall and I had met – young poets in Brisbane – and we decided to co-edit a brave new anthology of the recent Australian verse. It's the sort of thing young poets always talk about, and we were determined to make it more than talk. Our anthology, *New Impulses in Australian Poetry*, did come out – but in 1967, five years later, which perhaps indicates the slow pace of activity in that period. The old CLF (Commonwealth Literary Fund) had a form of "guarantee against loss" to Australian publishers and this was the only way poetry could be brought out in this country at the time; and the CLF had hesitated and hesitated, claiming our collection was too long, that new poetry should be given only in a condensed or token form. Even so, when it did finally get through the cumbersome machinery of patronage that then operated, our anthology was still the first to give major representation to such poets as Les Murray, Geoffrey Lehmann, Kath Walker (Oodgeroo Noonuccal) and Gwen Harwood.

In the course of our searches, Rodney obtained the address of another apparently new local poet: one Francis Geyer. I had already noted Geyer's work, particularly in the annual anthology produced by the journal *Australian Letters* in Adelaide. In the brief biographical notes at the back of the journal Geyer had written: "I am a musician, particularly interested in Bartok and have spoken English fluently from about the age of seven." Aha, I had thought, someone of Hungarian origin obviously, one who shares my passion for Bela Bartok,

and a poet! Also, as Rodney discovered, one with a Brisbane address, in Camp Hill.

We decided to make an expedition in my car to meet this neighbour poet, choosing the next available Saturday afternoon.

It was a typical little Queensland house on stilts. There was a neat garden with the size of lawn that we took for granted but which bespoke a full weekend of mowing every other week. We were greeted at the front door by a tidy, pert white-haired lady who said her name was Mrs Foster. No, unfortunately Mr Geyer was not in this weekend, he was the boarder, he worked... oh somewhere away... I think Mrs Foster might have suggested he was a Surveyor's Assistant, something like that, something which meant he was hardly ever home.

Yes, she looked after his mail for him. Yes, she would tell him we had called, would we like to come in, have a cup of tea in the kitchen, she had a few things she would perhaps show us that might be of interest and yes, she did know that Mr Geyer did write poetry... and we were poets, too, wasn't that nice, Mr Geyer would be very interested to hear about us, what were our names?

She fussed over us and provided us with cake and sweet cups of tea. We talked on about what we were doing, who we were, where we had published (she kept prodding us), and who we were thinking of including in our proposed anthology. "I do hope you will have something of Gwen Harwood", she couldn't resist suggesting.

The penny dropped. Gwen Harwood had achieved national notoriety in 1961, in the pages of the *Bulletin*. It was a period of transition for that paper, when it had been taken over by Australian Consolidated Press. Douglas Stewart, the literary editor for twenty years, had gone; and I am not sure if Vincent Buckley his successor had yet been appointed. At any rate, in 1961 two sonnets by a frequently published poet of the time, Walter Lehmann, appeared in the *Bulletin*: 'Eloise to Abelard' and 'Abelard to Eloise'. They were quite good poems, I remember them. However, a day after that week's issue of the *Bulletin* had appeared in the newsstands of the nation, I was in a country town outside Ipswich doing an audit of the books of the local Shire Council when the Shire Clerk rushed in. "Race out and buy up every copy of this week's *Bulletin*," he cried. "They're already selling for ten pounds each!"

"Why so?" I demanded.

"There's these acrostic poems in it, and there's a four-letter word!" It seems unimaginable from this point in time to think back into the repressive and censored world of the 1960s. The scandal of a four-letter word appearing in public print broke all the rigid conventions, conventions that had been set in concrete in our culture. Even if the word appeared in this case as an acrostic, an arcane literary device whereby the first letter of each line reveals, vertically, some hidden message. In the case of Walter Lehmann, the acrostic read: "So long *Bulletin*. Fuck all editors".

The Shire Clerk told me, knowledgeably, that this Walter Lehmann had had some sort of fight with the *Bulletin* staff, hence this shocking verbal crossword.

A fortnight later the *Bulletin* produced an issue containing an extraordinary and elaborate apology, begging the sensibilities of delicate readers not to be too horrified by this heinous trick which the new editor, untried in these matters, had allowed to slip through his censor's watchdog guard.

What was more, it was revealed, "Walter Lehmann" was the *nom-de-plume* for a woman. Gwen Harwood.

The thought of all poetry editors now scanning each poem submitted for subversive acrostics was irresistible to me. I submitted a poem of my own, 'Return is not Again', which contained its own acrostic, "Kiss Gwennie where she says" (this being a quotation from one of the songs in Dylan Thomas's *Under Milk Wood*, then enormously popular). My poem was published, but no-one rushed out to buy ten-pound copies.

Gwen Harwood, in that one act of literary sabotage, was thrust forward as a poet to watch. Perhaps to watch carefully. Certainly to watch with anticipation. Hers was the most successful literary hoax since the 'Ern Malley' poems of the 1940s. It was rumoured that she had written an incisively funny set of parodies of many of the "established" Australian poets, based on the old children's nurs-

ery tune: 'Round and round the mulberry bush'. These were circulating only among friends and initiates.

In the event Rodney and I soon joined the initiates, with the receipt of the now-famous Gwen Harwood "Sappho Cards" – postcards made from carefully selected collages of nineteenth-century illustrations from picture papers and speech "bubbles" from contemporary comics. Hobart, where Gwen Harwood lived, seemed to be a centre of prodigious activity in the production of these cards. Once Mrs Foster had raised the name of Gwen Harwood in her kitchen in Camp Hill on that afternoon, even as Rodney and I heard the name drop, her game was up. She gleefully had to confess to being the front person (I am sure she would have said "front man" with proper relish) for Gwen Harwood in her latest pseudonym. Then she proceeded to regale us with all kinds of stories about her daughter, her childhood, her family, her adored dad, her children and husband and all her tricks as a young thing, the way she haunted Toowong Cemetery, her talent as a pianist... The kitchen hummed with pride and satisfaction.

Rodney and I eventually walked back to my car, elated: the afternoon had turned up rather more than we had planned. Now the beginning of a long correspondence with Gwen, by both of us, began. Walter Lehmann and Francis Geyer had been uncovered –

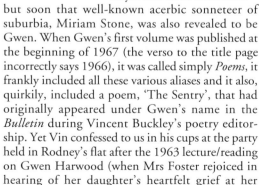

Gwen Harwood with the last known ink-mark of Timothy Kline

but soon that well-known acerbic sonneteer of suburbia, Miriam Stone, was also revealed to be Gwen. When Gwen's first volume was published at the beginning of 1967 (the verso to the title page incorrectly says 1966), it was called simply *Poems*, it frankly included all these various aliases and it also, quirkily, included a poem, 'The Sentry', that had originally appeared under Gwen's name in the *Bulletin* during Vincent Buckley's poetry editorship. Yet Vin confessed to us in his cups at the party held in Rodney's flat after the 1963 lecture/reading on Gwen Harwood (when Mrs Foster rejoiced in hearing of her daughter's heartfelt grief at her demise) that 'The Sentry' was in fact his (Vin's) own poem, written "in the style of Gwen Harwood" to see if readers would spot the work as a parody. ("It's a great poem", I had said tactfully.)

When it was finally published, Gwen Harwood's *Poems* clearly reinforced Buckley's early claim, in that 1963 lecture, that she was one of the outstanding poets in Australia. Vin had come to Queensland for that lecture with what I felt was a sort of Melbourne aggressiveness to make this assertion. This was at a time when Gwen Harwood was little known (except within the ranks of those determined to keep abreast of the latest developments) and when she had published no book. Vin's pronouncement was also a direct challenge to the great reverence held for the work of Judith Wright; it was thrust deliberately in one of the strongholds of Judith Wright's following. Vin had already taken some terse swipes at Judith Wright in his collection *Essays in Poetry, Mainly Australian* – a pivotal book. but I am sure his real intention, in that 1963 lecture, was to herald the arrival of a new, and Queensland-born, poet of brilliance. And that he could not resist the temptation of tightening the ropes around his own personal boxing ring.

The poems which helped to establish Gwen Harwood's reputation are her sequences about eccentric European intellectuals: in *Poems* the character of "Eisenbart" is a complex and savage lecher and thinker; in *Poems Volume Two* the drunken musician and teacher "Kröte" offers a more satiric and playful scope. And perhaps the most frequently anthologised of Gwen Harwood's poems of this period is one of her "suburban sonnets" – 'In the Park' – which has an extraordinarily powerful ending, where the mother realises of her children "They have eaten me alive".

Yet for me it is Gwen's "hospital poems" that strike an extraordinary chord. In Australian poetry only the "hospital poems" of Kenneth Mackenzie (which seem wilfully neglected) and also those of Francis Webb can be compared with those of Gwen Harwood. Webb's hospital poems are very special, they are amongst his greatest works; but Gwen Harwood in her poems of suffering and survival reveals an immense capacity for power and precision. Her most recent collection, *Bone Scan*, has, as it were, significantly developed this aspect of her writing. One of the interesting consequences of *Bone Scan* is that it throws a new light on the hospital poems of the earlier volumes; and that they thereby gain a new, more informed, emphasis.

My involvement with the uncovering of Gwen Harwood's many faces had its final twist in 1969.

"Just when you think it's safe to go back into the water..." In that year I was editing a new anthology for Sull Books – *Australian Poetry Now* – as various a haul of immediately contemporary writing as I could gather. One of the emerging poets who took my eye was a certain Timothy Kline. I got his address easily enough. It was Tasmania.

Oho?

Kline had not yet put together an individual collection of his work – even though by 1969 the University of Queensland Press was embarking on their hugely successful "Paperback Poets" series at $1 a volume, and new writers were suddenly in demand. Indeed, UQP had approached him for a manuscript. Now, it was not difficult for me to go through the various literary journals and assemble a good number of Kline's poems. But when I had done this, something curious emerged: it was one thing to read the poems individually as they had been published through journals and newspapers, it was another thing to read them as a group. What struck me, apart from the aptness of expression, was a unity of voice, of tone. When I looked closer, there was more than a whiff of something else: it was the cadence of Gwen Harwood.

I wrote Gwen a letter making heavy hints about "Tiny Tim a.k.a. Timothy Kline". She succumbed with graciousness and confessed all. She even sent me a photograph of herself walking smartly along a Hobart street carrying a briefcase. On the footpath behind the briefcase was a large spreading stain. "Last ink-mark of the late Timothy Kline", she wrote.

Not long afterwards I became rather abashed at uncovering this fresh face of Gwen Harwood. There may have been many more poems by "Timothy Kline" that might have happened but now were aborted, just like that ink-stain. And so I wrote to Gwen reassuringly and confirmed that "Tiny Tim" would be included in my anthology, now all the more rich and quizzical for the trick. Gwen replied with Timothy Kline's 'Statement of Poetics' (something I requested of all contributors) in rhymed heroic couplets. I thought this was just a little conspicuous so I printed the couplets as a straight prose block of words. The rhymes were available to those with ears. One reviewer of the anthology when it came out gurgled with glee that I held been tricked by a "phoney poet"...

The real question over Gwen Harwood persists. The delicious part of the question is: has she invented further *noms-de-plume*, fresh disguises? If so, who are they? The disturbing part of the question is: has some valuable element of her means of expression been stifled? The poems written by her under her various disguises are sufficiently powerful and original to make one aware that they add something crucial to the person we know as "Gwen Harwood". Sometimes the elements of play can be very serious indeed.

Gwen's mother Mrs Foster in her old age was well into tricks and jokes and liveliness... Has her daughter, more than twenty years after that last disclosure of false identity and true invention as "Timothy Kline", knitted yet another poet, or several, into our literary seams? It's possible – except that by the 1990s, with the relentless proliferation of literary conferences, Writers' Weeks and Word Festivals, there is hardly a poet in the country who has not been forced to face up to an audience in person.

Gwen Harwood several times over the years visited me in Brisbane. "Ah, Paradise!" she called out fondly – even though the paradise of her Brisbane had been pasted over by the modern city, and even though the invention of her personal paradise, as Brisbane, involved those necessary long years of exile in Tasmania. In that special paradise of her imagination, I think of her various personae as attendant angels, no matter how many there are or if more than one might have escaped my net. If ever there is a full and final Gwen Harwood *Collected Poems*, I hope they all nestle in; and are recognised; and are counted.

Gwen Harwood died in 1995; a *Collected Poems* was published by OUP in 1991. Tom Shapcott is an Australian poet and novelist. He has published 6 novels and 14 volumes of poetry, and received the Struga Gold Wreath Award (Macedonia) in 1989. This article first appeared in *Biting the Bullet* (Secker & Warburg, 1991).

Snodgrass on Guard

by Jo Shapcott

The whole of the truth lies in the presentation.
– Joseph Conrad

IN THE SPRING of 1993 I met W. D. Snodgrass at the Craiova poetry festival in Romania. One night, as we sat drinking beer outside in the town square, I asked him about *Remains*, my favourite of his books. He first published it in 1970 under another identity, calling himself S. S. Gardons. The name is not merely an anagram, not merely Snodgrass backwards (almost) or even "Snodgrass sideways", as the man himself described it[1], but a disguised way of alerting us to the protective mask ("guard on" or like the French, *garder*).

Remains was published complete with a spoof biography in which the supposed author is given a humble background any poet would die for and a life story which culminates in a mysterious disappearance. The mask is both fun and deliberately unconvincing:

S. S. Gardons lived most of his life in and near Red Creek, Texas. For years he worked as a gas station attendant, though he took a few university classes in Houston, and later became an owner of a cycle shop. Also a musician, he played lead guitar in a well-known rock group, Chicken Gumbo. This sequence of poems was collected by his friends after his disappearance on a hunting trip in the mountains. From the condition of his abandoned motorcycle, it was impossible to determine whether he suffered foul play, was attacked by animals, or merely became confused and lost, or perhaps fell victim to amnesia. At present the case is listed as unsolved.[2]

Snodgrass was modestly surprised to find a British poet intrigued by *Remains* and went on to tell me of yet another identity, Will McConnell, who published a few poems in magazines in the 1950s. I later came to suspect there was at least one more: Kozma Petrovitch Prutkov. A poem first published in *The Hudson Review*, under Snodgrass's name, carried the note "from the Russian of Kozma Petrovitch Prutkov".[3]

The same poem, 'The Mother', later appeared in the anthology by Robert Pack and Donald Hall, *New Poets of England and America,* but this time under Gardons' name[4]. You wouldn't need to be Hercule Poirot to make the connection. Snodgrass, by design not chance, laid a trail of clues to the true identity of Gardons which anyone interested at all in contemporary poetry could have spotted at the time without difficulty. Another monster of a clue came in Snodgrass's own biographical details as they appeared in the anthology *A Controversy of Poets*, where he was described as being "deeply influenced by the Texas poet, S. S. Gardons".

Both Snodgrass and Gardons appeared in the Pack and Hall anthology in separate, apparently unrelated sections, causing some grumpiness among commentators. One found fault with Snodgrass for getting twice his share of space in the anthology by these devious means and went on to make the ungenerous hint that Gardons had been invented as a younger man in order that Snodgrass might remain unfairly eligible for various literary opportunities on offer for writers under-forty[5]. When I got to this point in the review I began to wonder whether S. S. Gardons was in fact the author of it, too, under another name.

Back in the Romanian town square, I asked Snodgrass the real reason he had adopted the identities of McConnell and Gardons. His answer was simple. He wanted to protect family members who might identify themselves or others in the poems. And there is no doubt that *Remains* is a powerful work. It is a sequence of eight poems focusing on the death of a sister – "Flowers like a gangster's funeral;/Eyeshadow like a whore". ('Viewing the Body') – in which the characters of mother and father are drawn with unsuppressed rage combined with wonderful artistry. The fact that the identity of Gardons would have been well known among writers and critics wouldn't necessarily have hampered the effectiveness of the mask outside the literary world. From Snodgrass's comment in the notes to his *Selected Poems: 1957–1987* we can infer that the death of his parents released him from the necessity for disguise: "*Remains* was first published in a small, letterpress edition under the pseudonym S. S. Gardons by the Perishable Press in 1970. After the death of my parents, a new edition was issued by BOA Editions, Ltd. under my own name".[6]

Disguise just for the hell of it, and disguise to protect. But could there be even more behind creating a Texan gas-pumping version of yourself in reverse? In his remarkable essay on the imposter-poet, 'Snodgrass's Borrowed Dogs', the American poet David Wojahn places *Remains* at the pinnacle of Snodgrass's work and argues that the disguise is essential to the book, at the heart of it, serving "to enhance the ... tension, complexity, and ultimate artistic success".[7]

If this is true it might seem strange that W.D. Snodgrass is known most of all as the poet of sincer-

ity; he is the writer of *Heart's Needle*, the book which famously nudged Robert Lowell towards *Life Studies*. "I am left, then", said Snodgrass in his 1959 essay 'Finding a Poem', "with a very old-fashioned measure of a poem's worth – the depth of its sincer-ity".[8] But all poets constantly devise ways to stretch their potential, to step outside their own limitations. Snodgrass acknowledged that the invention of S. S. Gardons had had this effect on his work and he was convinced the transformation was quite visible in the *Remains* poems. *Remains*, he said, "started out being quite similar to the *Heart's Needle* poems, but the last ones are really quite different... You just change".[9]

Snodgrass has stepped into the shoes of a number of poets as a fine translator. "Joyous inventions" was a term he used to describe translations of poetry and a variety of inventions have followed in his own poems. A more-or-less closely related character "W. D.", sometimes called "The Poet", peppers his later poems. Snodgrass's controversial work *The Hitler Bunker* is peopled with famous characters, including Hitler, who speak to us directly from the last days of the Third Reich. And although I'm not aware of any recent versions of S. S. Gardons in Snodgrass's work, it doesn't do to be too complacent. After all, "You just change".

1. *American Poetry Observed: Poets on their Work*, ed Joe David Bellamy, University of Illinois Press, Urbana and Chicago, 1984
2. Quoted in *The Poetry Of W.D. Snodgrass: Everything Human*, edited by Stephen Haven, The University of Michigan Press, Ann Arbor, 1993, p 67
3 and 5. 'Snodgrass Peoples His Universe', George Monteiro in *The Poetry Of W.D. Snodgrass: Everything Human*, edited by Stephen Haven, The University of Michigan Press, Ann Arbor, 1993, pp 39-40
4. *New Poets of England and America: Second Selection*, edited by Donald Hall and Robert Pack, Meridian Books, New York, 1962
6. *Selected Poems* 1957-1987, W.D. Snodgrass, Soho Press, New York, 1987
7. 'Snodgrass's Borrowed Dogs: S.S. Gardons and Remains', David Wojahn in *The Poetry Of W.D. Snodgrass: Everything Human*, edited by Stephen Haven, The University of Michigan Press, Ann Arbor, 1993, pp 196-213
8. 'Finding a Poem', W.D. Snodgrass, printed as an addendum in The Marvell Press edition of *Heart's Needle*, Yorkshire, 1960

Quadrophrenia

by Adam Thorpe

FERNANDO PESSOA

The Book of Disquietude

Translated by Richard Zenith
Carcanet, £9.95
ISBN 1 85754 301 7

Selected Poems

Translated by Jonathan Griffin
Penguin, £6.99
ISBN 0 14 018845 2

A Centenary Pessoa

Edited by Eugenio Lisboa with L.C. Taylor
Carcanet, £25
ISBN 0 85635 936 X

BY CANCELLING HIMSELF, Fernando Pessoa hoped to discover his essential self, even if that essentialism admitted absence or non-existence. He thought of writing as an act of faking, and belief itself as believing in disbelief or in what one doesn't believe. Truth is silent, soundless, beyond cognition. In one poem, 'I Still Keep', he pictures reality's "false delight" as the yellow petals around "the black centre that's all". In his vast fragmentary poetic fiction, *The Book of Disquietude*, he thinks of the countryside as only real when no one sees it – a reflection that was Emerson's and Hardy's before him. He talks of existence not only as a dream or reverie but as an "approximation" and his (or his persona's) writing as "scraps, fragments, excerpts of the non-existent".

To observe something is to renew and multiply it, and the same goes for the self – that illusion of completeness, dispersed through time and space, an "advent" rather than an end. Shadows feature strongly in Pessoa's work: shadows change or are extinguished with changes of light, and his work favours the nocturnal. Every moment of life (whatever illusory phenomenon the word "life" tries to evoke) shatters our sense of wholeness, and all that is left us is the power to gaze. This gazing may "perceive / In the shadow and its movement / What, in the other world, is meant / By that gesture which makes him live", yet elsewhere he notes how feeling

is like the sky, "Seen, nothing in it to see": the moment of intuition is itself speechless, like the heart's ache.

The only answer is to fake it, and in that faking to create a kind of para-feeling, painful or happy, which is neither the property of the poet nor of the reader. Pessoa is the stealthiest stalker of essential truth this century has known: by pretending he hasn't seen it, that there is in fact nothing to see, he might just catch it. To know what the trees are doing when no one is looking at them, he must pretend he isn't there, or isn't real, at the moment of the most intense attention. Thus every poem or fragment of prose is doomed to describe its own failure and fakery. The reader is left with a thrilling sense of absence that is not the complexity the intrusion of the poet has created, but the "truly simplest things" which the poem has failed to describe by describing them.

Pessoa does not believe in wholeness or unity, but in what literary theorists term "*différance*". Is there any connectedness across this *différance*? As his Bloom-like assistant bookkeeper puts it in *The Book of Disquietude*, wandering the vast lands of his own tedium: "I don't have any idea of myself, not even the kind that consists of the lack of an idea of myself. I'm a nomad of my consciousness of self. The herds of my inner riches slipped away in the first watch". Of course, Pessoa is not one poet but four. Fernando Pessoa, born 1888, the Anglophile and bilingual Portuguese writer from Durban who lived as a translator of commercial letters in Lisbon, enjoyed his white wine and tobacco and died in 1935 having never left the city for thirty years, leaving a trunk full of unpublished writings, is not Ricardo Reis (classically pagan, erudite), Alberto Caeiro (the ruthlessly *naïf* singer of Nature), or Alvaro de Campos (the dishevelled urban Dionysus). Neither is he quite Barnado Soares, humble assistant bookkeeper and composer of much of the vast *Book of Disquietude* – though Pessoa refers to Soares as a "mutilated" version of himself. But through the three "heteronyms" and the "semi-heteronym" of Soares, Pessoa stood sufficiently outside himself to start on the path to finding the heart's truth. This is not quite like the transcendental religious impulse: that presupposes a carnal self coherent enough to transcend. Though Pessoa certainly thought of Being as in some way carnal, he didn't fragment an ur-self to write what he wanted to write, so much as allow himself to be surprised by himself wearing a succession of masks.

(By happy coincidence, "Pessoa" is a derivation of the Latin *persona*, meaning a Roman theatre-mask.) Neither is this the deliberate pretence of a translated voice in order to say things one couldn't say otherwise in the "native" garb – as with Christopher Reid's Katerina Brac or Geoffrey Hill's Sebastian Arrurruz. It is, in the end, a Modernist act of defiant and passionate aporia.

It all happened in a rush as he stood at his sloping desk on the 8th of March 1914. Joyce had already started his multi-tongued odyssey and in three months an apparently secure continent would be suddenly shattered. Pessoa's audacious "sleight of words" started with Caeiro's superb paean to pastoral simplicity, 'The Keeper of Sheep', went on through Pessoa's 'Chuva Obliqua', Reis's strict Horatian metres and finally Campos's Whitmanesque Futurism in wildly free verse. Yet it arose out of a joke: an attempt to invent a bucolic poet for a friend's enjoyment. These four poets had complicated histories and relations with each other – Reis the pupil of Caeiro living in political exile in Brazil, Campos the Anglophile writing his memoir of the dead shepherd whose verse is a kind of primordial pre-verse, Pessoa released by the three others into the kind of poet who could write stealthily beautiful love-poems (as perhaps Eliot was released by Prufrock):

> Audible smile of the leaves,
> Just the wind at that place,
> If I gaze at you and you gaze
> At me, who is it that smiles
> First? The first to smile laughs.
> Laughs, and gazes suddenly
> So as not to gaze,
> At where can be sensed in leaves
> The noise of the breeze as it goes.
> All is breeze and disguise.
>
> (from 'Audible Smile of the Leaves',
> trs Jonathan Griffin)

The Book of Disquietude is redolent with the tobacco smells of Lisbon, the humdrum offices and cafés and bookshops of its pre-war self, as much as of the disquietude that haunts Kafka's work, or the metaphysical pessimism of the late exile-philosopher, Cioran. Kafka and Pessoa and Cioran are exiles in their own cities, literally and metaphysically. Kafka the Jew in Prague, Cioran the Romanian in Paris, Pessoa the English-educated arrival from Durban who opted to make himself invisibly Portuguese. Exile involves role-playing, the adoption of masks, because one sees as in a mirror the futility of one's own notion of what it means to be understood.

Pessoa claimed to be nothing but his writing, but wrote at night so as to be able to have an exterior life. In this exterior life he could enter into the humblest and least phenomena – that which is literally on the edge of not-being-seen-at-all. Soares sits in his empty office and watches the sunlight crawl across the bare floor, just as Kafka (a little more daring) let the ribbon of a passing dress run through his fingers outside his father's shop. Soares/Pessoa finds this particularity morbidly amusing, too, and can deflect it onto himself: the boss's girlfriend ringing just when the bookkeeper is in the middle of "my meditation on the most asexual period of an aesthetic and intellectual theory". In the end, the lines between the exterior and the interior are blurred, are fake, perhaps do not exist at all, as they do not exist in dreams. As Octavio Paz writes in *A Centenary Pessoa* (a joyful *Festschrift*): "The world of Pessoa is neither this world nor the other". Yet one comes away from these books rinsed by an intense sense of Being, more "alert" to its surprises.

Shame on us that the Penguin *Selected Poems* is the only easily-available entry into Pessoa's works (with odd omissions of important poems but a fine translator in the late Jonathan Griffin): the French editions of each of the heteronyms run to hundreds of pages. Now at least we have the complete *Book of Disquietude* (there is also the Serpent's Tail edition of 1992, incidentally), which ranks as one of the most important poetic fictions of the century – and one of the most simply enjoyable, too. James Greene has produced some singing translations of the poems (*The Surprise of Being*, Angel Classics, 1986) and The Menard Press published Griffin's bilingual edition of *Message* in 1992. Message is an epic poem that reinvents and then dissolves the myth of Portugal, opening with Europe "propped upon her elbows" and ending with his country scattered and become "fog". It was the only book published in his lifetime: the rest was found stuffed into a large trunk after his death, and is still being sorted by scholars from the fragmentary muddle that was, for this extraordinary poet, the essential quality of existence.

Adam Thorpe's third novel and third book of poetry are forthcoming from Cape.

GEORGE SZIRTES

THE GARDEN OF EARTHLY DELIGHTS

In the garden of earthly delights a maid sings
in the moonlight and hands escape from their
supporting roles
to act out erotic fantasies as lovers or wings,
or fish in sensually drifting shoals
of light and coloured air.

A frogman appears in the deep like a drowned
monster pulling faces through his goggles.
A plump red heart
floats above a mannequin to the sound
of drums. Two old grotesques start
a fight. One struggles

with the other, they knock their heads together,
rolling over and over. It's all about money
and lust – what else is there?
Scraps of cloth, bits of old shoe leather,
stuff from the junkshop, all things spare
and cheap and funny.

All this in a tiny theatre the size of a man's head,
a man with a big head, a completely outrageous
capacious and outsize
head who is telling a story composed of fraying thread
held together by conventions, tricks and lies,
the discarded pages

of ancient directories to the business of living.
The grown ups are being graceful to amuse
their notional child.
They are trying to impose order on the unforgiving
minute. Like poetry, it is the formal dance of the wild,
news which stays news.

JAMES SUTHERLAND-SMITH
ODYSSEUS' LAST VOYAGE

You live in a village called Entropy,
A settlement that has grown up since I left.
There is little time left available for work;
All day to bat an eyelid, a kiss can take all night.
And in the summer heat those seeds blown hard
For dandelion clocks float down so timelessly.

There are visions, not stars scattered like brilliants,
But the sky lacy with histories of star position.
At dawn the sun rises as a pillar of light
Then all day ribbons over us, a silken dragon
Until it vanishes as in a nursery rhyme
Dragging its tail behind. I have grown so old;

Salt crystals round my joints so I cannot leap,
Salt-speckled my hair and beard, salty my speech.
Sweet-talk is not listened to these days
Above the ever-rising roar of nonsense.
There is so much disorder to set aside,
So much energy required with many a word

Laid to waste before sense comes through loud and clear.
I have returned to the point where I once believed
You would make me always young and ill at ease,
(Elsewhere my tongue comfortable with the syllables
Of languages got as I dawdled twenty years
In the troughs and swells of the seven seas.)

Yes, I have returned to the point where I once believed
Lodestones began, where everything must reverse:
The blown dandelion seed to pause and then
Fly upwards to the stalk, your eyes to close,
Your head to tilt back again through ecstasy.
But no, my love, such hope like sea spray will disperse.

Sun, moon and stars will dwindle to become alike;
A salt glitter on the near total cold.
And this hand I have stretched out to yours
Now slows as though at least the body understands
That a turning point will neither come nor go,
That such events do not occur. My hand hovers:

It neither reaches out to touch nor withdraws.

SARAH CORBETT
PYLONS

In the fields beyond the town
the pylons have wings. They grew in the
                              night,
cocooned then flowered;
from our beds we listened
to the steel-edged moans of their making.

Now we have gathered,
a carnival crowd drawn
by the snap and whiplash of lines;
we watch as they heave to the sun,
flock in the sky and darken us.

Yet we are hopeful for them,
we send them our children's names
as if it was us that set them loose,
and, in doing so, wonder where they will
                              land
and who will find them.

Nearly gone, they flash,
quick lit tapers burning out
in the last of the day's light,
their scattered messages falling
as soft rain on upturned faces.

WAYNE BURROWS
A PARABLE

If I start to climb
the apple tree
and swing out
from a lichened bough
by the three
middle fingers
of a single hand,
defy gravity
say, twenty feet
from earth
and slop bravado
like apple-juice
in the sunlit leaves,
I'll be OK.
But think: *You'll fall.*
It's slippery.
Break your neck/arms/legs,
and then . . .
Then my fingers feel
less secure,
the whole tree
delicately poised

on its root;
my arm grows tired,
shoulder strains,
the windfalls bruise
a long way down.
Fall off then, stupid.
At your age, you . . .
But I know no better.
I cling where air
and branches thin
to twigs and leaf-stalks,
nets of wood.
In a cobalt sky
I might fall through
with trails of cloud
and chimney-smoke,
birds and jetstreams,
kites, balloons,
I've access to vistas
almost mine
and listen, I tell you,
no way down.

JAYANTA MAHAPATRA
PERFORMANCE

So often I have thought of moving
the stars about in the skies
to lighten up the lives of the children,
and even thought I'd done it at times;
but then it was as if everybody
saw though it, saw through everybody else.
My look of conscientious purpose
dies on my son's door. And
when there is too much of my life to hide
I pretend that I do not know what I want,
making me nervous enough for me to shout
for my son. Or for the daughter I do not have.
But does anything I say or do matter,
if I risk nothing of my life?
This easy myth we live in,
my fate which like a summer koel, answers
my imitation of its calls through the warm nights.
Once my father said: If you work hard
there will be time enough to play later.
I don't know. If I think of him
I feel I am staring at the deep water
of his face with the look of one about to drown.
Here the children keep watching me
as though I had robbed them of their youth.
And the stars, mere fireworks in the skies
celebrating some childhood victory
whose sounds have been lost in the thickening air.

Note: The summer koel is a bird of the cuckoo family, inhabiting leafy gardens, groves and
woodland in India. It becomes noisy and is seen and heard with the advance of summer. Its
fluty double call has a haunting quality and, when imitated, responds by familiar crescendo
calls. The bird is silent in winter and so is recorded as absent. Hence, a summer koel.

RUTH PADEL
WATERLOO BRIDGE

Part of me is sure you must deserve
All I can throw at you, and more.
The rest of me believes you're thoughtless, yes,
But also anxious, loving, seven skins too few,
And so – so unaware you make me weep.
You never see the choice I see you making
Week by week. Your hunting song
In geisha city taking pride of place.
(or am I wrong?) As if there's something
In you that had never had enough ("I'm starved
Of love"), you've had to keep on seeking.
Pan in love with a green elusive Echo.
A recidivist lemon sherbert, depending on
Exposure to the public air, for fizz.

We're different species. Never mind the odd unkind
Reproach: you give me what a river gives a city –
A heartline, for the palm of a closed-in hand.
Despite the shadowed banks (bloodclots
Tadpoling about through sagging veins,
The priest knifed at communion, bitter dying words
To a frightened wife), it's all here, all of it again,
And lifting when you're on the bridge.
You suddenly remember – Augustine to Hollywood –
Just what a city is. This human going-on at being grand.
The sea directive darkling at its centre, hung
With necklaces of light. Different ways
Of knowing, flowing within my own. Like you.
Like you again. The living, generous night.

The Lovely Ruse

MARK DOTY IN CONVERSATION WITH CAROLE SATYAMURTI.
AN EDITED VERSION OF AN INTERVIEW RECORDED FOR
SOUTH AFRICAN RADIO IN NOVEMBER 1996

Carole Satyamurti: I suppose that, in Britain at least, you are primarily known for poetry that has been written out of the experience of loss, particularly loss arising from the Aids epidemic – a statement which perhaps makes your work sound rather mournful and solemn. And yet it is anything but that. One of the qualities I admire in your poetry is the way you weave together grief and affirmation and heighten both in the process. I'm thinking of the poem 'Brilliance', for instance, in which a dying man – and you in writing about him – wrestles with the question of what it would mean to form a new attachment to something when it has so soon to be given up.

Mark Doty: That is a poem which in fact comes out of a rather positive story arising from the epidemic. A friend of mine who found herself comfortably retired, devoting her time to a few poems and to bird-watching, began to change her life by working as a volunteer for a man living with Aids. She soon found that, rather than just going once a week, she was seeing him two or three times a week and soon every day. And when he died she became a volunteer, working with someone else, and soon found herself the director of the volunteer training project for the state of Rhode Island in the US. So, this is one of those stories that arises out of a time of great difficulty when meaning is found – a new meaning is found – in a life.

CS: In 'Brilliance', as in so many others of your poems, one sees a succession of layers. At the end, the idea is entertained that the man might, at the moment of dying, pass into the life of the last object of his attachment – a goldfish – as a legendary Zen master became a fawn at his death. Initially that struck me as an expression of hopefulness, but I then thought that, for the Zen master, becoming a fawn is a kind of failure. It undoes his life's work of detachment. I wonder whether you mean the reader to have that paradoxical response?

MD: I do, indeed. It seems to me that reality is always so marbled between the light and dark, between the positive and the negative. And I wouldn't want to write a poetry which could easily come to rest in one point of view. The dialogue between attachment and detachment, the praise of involvement in the world, placed next to our desire, our also human desire, to let go, seems to me where the life of the poem resides. Poetry for me is always a process of inquiry. If I knew what I thought, if I knew what I felt about what compels me in the world, I doubt that I would write a poem. That part of our minds which makes metaphor proceeds ahead of us, and the metaphors seem to know more than we do about our emotional lives, about our ideas. What I see first is the vessel which contains feeling and thinking, and my work as a poet is to, as it were, lean against the given, or put pressure upon those images that strike me, in order to ask them to yield their meaning. So I almost always begin with description and find myself moving from description into questioning and meditation, which in turn lead to the poem's larger dimensions. If that process isn't completed, the poem usually isn't completed either. The world doesn't need another description from me! I hope that what I can do is use that quality of observation as a departure point to talk about those things that concern me most profoundly and therefore, one hopes, might also matter to a reader.

CS: Yes. You start with the object, and the reader's attention is drawn to the object. It's only by the end of the poem that we know that this is – also – a metaphor. A poem that seems to exemplify this wonderfully is 'Difference' in which close attention to jellyfish and the different objects they can resemble moves into a meditation on the shape-shifting properties of language. When one does this, the evocation of the object and what it opens out into, what it stands for, have both to work to their ultimate degree, don't they?

MD: Yes, I think so. We don't respond to abstractions as such. If I say the word "love", if I say the word "grief" or "regret" or "memory", those are evocative to a point but they can't give us the textured, complicated sense of reality which those terms can when they are allied with things, with the physical. I feel a kinship both to William Carlos Williams' statement, "no ideas but in things", and also to the concomitant notion of Wallace Stevens, "no things but in ideas". And for me, I want the inner life and the outer life, the idea and the object, to be as fused as I can possibly make them, because it seems to me that that's the way I can most render what it's like to perceive reality.

CS: Your work has evoked some extreme responses – from very high praise (and prizes) to the kind of reaction epitomised by John Hartley Williams' review of *My Alexandria,* in this magazine. Do you have any thoughts about why that might be?

MD: First of all, I'm grateful there *is* a critical discussion about my work; any writer is lucky to have that, even if the experience is not always an enjoyable one. That said, I would add that I find some sorts of reviews much more interesting and useful than others. It seems to me that the reviewer's work is to develop a line of thinking, an argument about the art, which uses the particular text at hand as a departure point. I am more interested in this argument than I am in whether the reviewer finds the book good or bad. The reviews of my work have been more noticeably various in Britain than in the US. I don't claim to understand this, but I have two theories about it. First, American reviewing, especially in the poetry world, is quite different. There is so little of it that I think we're inclined to review books we care about and leave the rest to gather dust in silence. We don't have the kind of "no holds barred" reviewing tradition which prevails here. I suspect that those who dislike my work in the US have mostly simply put their energies elsewhere. I don't know if this is a good thing or a bad thing. It saddens me that we don't have the intensity of debate which you have here, but I do not regret the absence of the tone of rancour I sometimes note in the discussion.

CS: Do you think that some of that rancour relates to the particular sensibility from which you write?

MD: The intensity of response over here suggests that my work has, as Madonna likes to say,

"pushed some buttons". It would be presumptuous of me as an outsider to suggest just what nerve I've struck, but perhaps it's not inappropriate to raise some questions. Does it have to do with the uses and value of the autobiographical? With intimacy or emotional directness? A perceived quality of accessibility, or the absence of certain forms of irony? The willingness to make statements in a rather public way, to claim for the poem that sort of authority? The tone of some reviews has led me to think that my work is being used as part of a conversation which does not concern me exactly, but to which my poems must lend themselves.

CS: Much of the intimacy and directness in your work concerns grief, and I suppose that grief is something that provides the impulse for many people, not just poets, to write – to put pen to paper. I've heard you say that, for you, writing about loss is helpful, not because it solves anything, but because it provides a container, a shape, for the emotion.

MD: Yes, I think one of the most difficult things about intense feeling is that such states of mind, when we are shattered by loss, feel so oceanic, so without edges or limits. Maybe one of the reasons that we reach for poetry in times of strong feeling is that not only does it seem to express our feeling but it requires us to stand back, just a bit, at a time when it's terribly, terribly difficult to achieve any kind of distance. When you make a poem, you are always paying attention to the shaping of language, to the form – those dimensions of craft which are, in and of themselves, a way of standing at a little distance from what it is you are saying. That's why writing in a journal vents one's feelings but doesn't really make one feel very much better: it doesn't offer us that kind of distance. The making of a work of art out of difficulty not only expresses how we feel but can be something given to another person. It can help to lift us out of the terrible solitude of grief and of loss into a sense of community, because when feeling is crafted into an artefact in language, it can be in some way shared between people. A connection can be made. There's something about having our feelings given form in the world, our experiences mirrored for us, that is, I believe, necessary to the human.

CS: Perhaps that goes back to our earliest babyhood when the mother can represent that kind of offering of containment, and then language itself becomes a way of containing and giving shape to chaotic feeling.

MD: It also goes back to our first sketches on the walls of the cave, our pictographs, those images of humankind which show us who we are.

CS: One of the things that strikes me about your use of language is some resonance of Gerard Manley Hopkins. I make that connection because in your poetry there is so much of the language of light – of light on surfaces – a rapturous immersion in contemplation of those surfaces and that light.

MD: Thank you! I love the dazzled surfaces of Hopkins' poems. I think of myself as a frustrated painter. So that kind of interest in colour, and in shimmer, and in the surfaces of things surely connects to that. I also think of myself as a frustrated singer. So the music of the poems in a way is an attempt to perform an aria. Perhaps what we do is fold our unrealised potential selves into whatever work we choose.

CS: Am I right in seeing in many of your poems – I think, for instance, of the title poem, 'Atlantis' – a suggestion of some sort of redemption, some transcendence of the fact of death, that comes from connectedness with the natural world?

MD: We're always looking for ways to understand our mortality, for ways to confront the fact of limit. I think, in a way, that many of my poems from the last two volumes are failed negotiations with the fact of loss. Because all negotiations with the fact of loss are doomed to fail. They are temporary stays against time. But it is that act of negotiating, it is by that act of bargaining, if you will, with time, that we make our mark in the world.

CS: Yes. I wonder if you'd see that as your central theme. Do you think that, in one way or another that is what you return to?

MD: Well, I think so. I am fascinated by evanescence, by the human gesture in the face of the great, overwhelming, implacable force of time. This morning I was lucky enough to walk through the first floor of the British Museum and to look at the extraordinary Egyptian figures who, even in their fragments, are still raising their hands toward us, whose gaze is still clear and straightforward after 5,000 years. Those works of art, contain, if you will, the humanity of their makers. I guess that what every artist would wish to join, in some fashion, is that human group.

CS: In my own work, I've often struggled with the ethical implications of turning something that has been catastrophic for someone else into art, and so into the stuff of poetic reputation. I wonder if this has been an issue for you, as you have written so much about death, and about the death of your own partner in particular.

MD: I'm glad that you raise this question. It's one that I've felt forced to confront over the course of a dozen years of writing poetry and prose which has often concerned the epidemic. I dislike the idea that there are things one shouldn't write about. I've written what my experience has demanded of me. The poems are products of a quest to understand the most difficult things in my life, a struggle to push up against the unsayable. I would prefer not to have been required to write about an epidemic, but the fact is that it has surrounded me and the people I love, and I would feel like a liar and a small man indeed if I didn't speak to these facts, these conditions. Obviously, some material is very challenging. When we write about suffering, we have to be hugely vigilant, since any trace of self-aggrandisement will seem enormous. It's the quality of engagement and of craft that makes the difference, not what the poem is "about". What I mean by the quality of engagement is that the poem embodies a genuine need to understand, that it is marked by compassion, and by an attempt to honour the experiences of others.

CS: One poem of yours that doesn't concern the epidemic but speaks directly out of gay experience, is 'Homo Will Not Inherit'. The poem represents your response to a situation where you're confronted with hostility and prejudice. You describe wandering around town and coming across a poster which says "Homo will not inherit. Repent and be saved". And your response to that is to say "I'll tell you what I'll inherit: the margins / which have always been mine..." It seems to me that there's a paradox that eventually emerges from the poem – through eloquently accepting a place on the margins, you redefine your place in such a way that it becomes the centre, or at least a centre. What strikes me as unusual about the poem is the anger in it, and the fierceness in it. Am I right in thinking that that's an unusual voice for you?

MD: It is, indeed. I said earlier that my poems

usually begin in not knowing what I'm struck by in an image, other than that it seems important to me. In this case, of course, I knew perfectly well what I felt about this outrageous street poster put up by someone on the fringe of the Christian Right. I felt that it registered with every act of oppression that I've known, which said that my desire, my identity, is one disapproved of by God, disapproved of by church and state. So I was filled with rage when I saw that poster and I wanted to give form to that rage, which has been a particular challenge for me, because I depend upon the energy of making discoveries to fuel the writing process. So I think it's much harder to begin from a point of self-knowledge, and particularly to begin from a point of anger, because it's such a volcanic, unbounded emotion. It destroys our distance, it spills out, it's like the lava flow of heat and lightning. The process of writing that poem was one, first of all, of pouring out that anger, simply letting it spill on to the page and then beginning to consider what might be made of it, which very much to me feels like the reading that you just offered. If we're pushed to the edges of our culture, if we're told that our feelings, our identities, are not part of the centre but are out there some place, on the outside, well, that means that we're granted some special kinds of perspectives, too. Because to be at a bit of a remove is to allow the values of the dominant culture not to be transparent for you, not to be just the element in which you live. These values seem more opaque, if you like, more visible. I have felt that many gifts have come to me, because of being a gay, American man, standing somewhat on the edge of my culture and thus given a different kind of possibility for vision. Whatever pushes us we can use, if we're lucky. If we have the strength and the opportunities then we can take our marginalisation, we can take whatever the difficult circumstances of our lives might be, and use those difficulties as a lens through which to see what matters. It's not the ostensible content that matters. It's the position in relation to the content that matters. Because we're all going to experience the loss of what we love, and we all in some ways don't fit in to the main stream. We're all in some way queer, on the edge, not quite who we're supposed to be. And so that common ground might be, paradoxically, something that links us as a community of strangers, a community of outsiders.

CS: I think that the way you treat landscape relates to that, because landscape, after all, is literally common ground, and it carries for all of us both shared and private meanings. It can give rise both to a sense of belonging and connectedness with other people, and also to complete solitariness. It seems to me that, in the particular place where you live, the part of the Massachusetts coast you write about, you have found your ideal landscape in the sense that this is a place where you can inexhaustibly contemplate the meanings that could be there.

MD: It's an extraordinary source of metaphor. I live on the very tip of Cape Cod, and there's a feeling of – as in many coastal places – a great fluidity and mutability. What was land at ten o'clock is sea at two o'clock. The fog rolls in and solid things disappear. That landscape of change, that border zone, has been a very rich source of metaphor for me about all kinds of change and borders.

CS: In 'Homo Will Not Inherit' you locate yourself at the margins, but in 'Fog Argument' you show us that different kind of edge. You show us, through close attention to the meeting and blurring of land and sea, that place where the edge – by implication, the self – fades out into nothing.

MD: That poem, like many in *Atlantis*, is an examination of the liminal, that edge where you can't tell endings from beginnings, life from death, the land from the sea. The question of where a self begins and ends seemed deeply pressurised to me, for obvious reasons – not merely philosophical any more, but a matter of the utmost urgency. What is this evanescent, loosely bounded thing we are? I think the two sections of that poem – the "argument" – represent opposing points of view about the limits of the self. It's an opposition with which I imagine I'll be wrestling all my life.

Mark Doty has published four collections of poetry, most recently *Atlantis*, published by Cape in 1996. His third book, *My Alexandria*, won the T. S. Eliot Prize in Britain and the National Book Critics Circle Award and the *Los Angeles Times* Book Award in America. Many of the poems explore the themes of love, loss and mortality, and were written out of the experience of the loss of his lover, Wally Roberts, from Aids. He has also written a prose memoir, *Heaven's Coast*, about that experience. A new collection, *Sweet Machine*, will be published by Cape in 1998.
With thanks to Sidney Buckland, who jointly planned and edited the interview, and to Hillary Keogh who directed the original broadcast.

MARK DOTY
LILIES IN NEW YORK

A drawing: smudged shadow, deep worked areas
of graphite rendering exactly a paper-wrapped
pot's particular folds, then each spiculate leaf,
their complex spiraling movement up the stem,
and the shining black nodes – seeds? – mounted
at the intersection of stalk and leaf: a work of
attention all the way up to the merest
suggestion of the three flowers,
a few rough unmodulated lines . . .

what's this about? Why,

up here where trumpeting
crowns all this darkness,
has the artist given up?

Exhaustion, since he's made such
a density of strokes below?
This page moves from deep,

pressured rendering
toward these slight gestures,
the flower merely sketched,

barely represented. Is it that
he wants us to think, *This is a drawing,
not a flower* and so reminds us

that the power of his illusion,
alive below the lily's neck,
is trickery? A formal joke,

airy fragility over such a field of marks,
warring masses, particulate suspensions
(lead, black chalk, charred – coal?

smoothed or scribbled or crosshatched
                              everywhere,
a made night); art's dialectic, the done
and undone, dirty worked spaces

and the clean blank gaze of the unfinished,
with all its airy invitations? Or is it
too much for him, to render that delicacy,

to bring the white throat out
of white paper, no hope of accuracy,
and so he makes this humble gesture

to acknowledge his own limitations,
because the lilies are perfect,
is that it, and what version

of their splendor would come any closer
than this wavering, errant line?
Or is he indifferent to flowering,

to culmination and resolution?
Would he rather remain with the push
of areas of darkness, the hustle

and dash of line, cacophony of pot
and stem, roiling swoops and scrawls
like clashing swathes of twilight,

furious? As if the frame
were filled with colliding expanses
of noise (traffic, sirens, some engine

hammering into the street below,
barking, airbrakes expelling their huge
mechanical tribute to longing,

arc of a train's passage and descent
below river), as if charcoal
were a medium of solidified sound,

is that it, which allowed the grind
and push of this city to render itself,
to pour through his hand

into its; own representation –
which does not hobble our apprehension
of the thing but honors its since it is

of the moment only, a singular
clarity and we understand, don't we,
that stasis is always a lie?

These only appear to be lilies,
this conflation of smudges,
but isn't the ruse lovely,

matter got up in costume as itself?
Isn't the dark carved now,
a moment, around the body

of the flower? New York's a clutch
in which these lilies are held,
let's say the drawing's subject

is Manhattan's grip, the instant
in which the city
constellates itself

around this vertical stroke
risen from a blur of florist's paper:
doesn't all of New York lean

into the hard black lines defining
stalk and leaf, a field of pressure
and distortion, a storm

billowing and forming itself
now around these shapes?
Isn't the city flower and collision?

Trumpet, trumpet, and trumpet:
now New York's a smear
and chaos of lilies, a seized whir,

burr and diminishment, a greased dark
clank of lilies which contains in itself
snowy throat and black crosshatched

field of atmosphere, scent
and explosion, tenderness
and history, all that's leaning

down into the delicate, nearly human skin,
pressing with its impossible weight,
despite which the mouth of the flower

– quick and temporary as
any gesture made by desire –
remains open. Lustrous,

blackening, open as if
about to speak. Open –
is that it? Out of these negotiations

arises a sketchy, possible
bloom, about to, going to,
going to be, becoming

open. And who could hope to draw that?

HARRY CLIFTON

THE COUNTRY OF STILL WATERS

I went again, from the country of flux,
    To the country of still waters.
An old stone house, a mother and two daughters
Laying the same ghost, unweaving the hex
Like retted flax. To have loved, to have hated –
Now, to watch the nettles at the gate,
The harbingers of desertion, stand and wait,
Indigenous, for all of us to die out.

The book of invasions shuts itself, and the powers
    Throw open their great houses
Once and for all. Admire their jugs, glazed ewers,
Untouchable, frozen in time. And the blunderbuss
On the mantelpiece, and the harpsichord
In the drawingroom. Stables and pigsties,
Servants' quarters. Gravel in the yard,
A whitewashed front. Admire it and do otherwise

For the workhouse slate is wiping itself clean,
    Finality reigns,
And every victim, every breaker of stone
Stands like a monument, now, to his own pain.
The Indian meal, the quart of buttermilk
In a tin mug, the dish on the spellbound table,
Numinous, its every grain unspilt,
Accounts for itself, in the completed fable.

Hurt consciousness, dazedly seeking out water –
    Maidenhead, luckless in love,
Now, second childhood. Mother, is it over
For the cloven halves of the apple, both your daughters?
Father, in your otherworld of quiet,
Where the great gentleness reigns, beyond spite
Or envy, higher than theodolite
Or spirit-level, tell me, do the grouse turn white

On the winter mountains? Now, you finally know,
    And the chain of expiation
Breaks forever. A pub, a filling station
In the wilderness. I park my car and go
On foot up an empty valley. Signs of habitation
Once, long ago. On ruined sills, a wren,
Territorial, marks its spaces out.
In the riverbed, a skitter of ghostly trout —

And there it is again, in all its flux,
    My country of still waters.
Racing light and shadow, mossgrown alders
Overhanging a waterfall. Sheep, transfixed
Or fleeing. Water, wood and stone,
A lost inheritance, physical, entire,
Disentangling itself from barbed wire,
Ridding itself of history, coming into its own.

The twenty-second Sunday in Ordinary Time —
    A chalice is raised
To Spirit in Matter. Silence, a chime,
While half the country bows its head and prays.
No past, no future. Stillness, a moratorium
Pausing over the mother and the daughters,
The old stone house, the country of still waters,
Wherever it may be, whenever it happens to come.

JOHN MOLE
SUMMER AFTERNOON

Voices from the dark square
of an upper window, somewhere
deep inside, invisible beauty
dancing on a quilted bed. How many
and what laughter? As I guessed
the quiet one was the loveliest
but would she step across the floor
to look down on the street? My car
was waiting merely for a friend
and not impatient. Hang around
like this, what else, the radio on
to catch the latest Beach Boys song
which caught her too. I wasn't wrong.

DAVID HART
ANGELICA AND BOB ON LINE

Angelica has crept out of bed and left early before getting on line.
She has missed the clip-art of a heart in the e-mail from Bob.
When Bob wakes with her gone it is from a dream of a woman
smashing through barbed wire towards the blue horizon.

Angelica in town swerves off into Uranus Precinct
and sees herself on video in the window of Dixon's.
Back at the home screen Bob frets and cries, *God only knows!*,
and for a moment this seems to be the breakthrough
he's been mousing his way through the fine folds of fields for.

The *Evening Echo*'s early edition is devoting half its front page
to a young woman covering her face caught on camera leaving
the Clearwater Centre but it isn't her. But this *is* her,
a photo from that happy summer scanned in on Bob's screen.
Enlarging it with zoom control he examines for intent
the edge of her smile. Elongating it a fraction
everything soon becomes clear. The screen doesn't lie
and he can read her lips. Her eyes, too, were somewhere else.

In her attic suite in the Delphi B & B seventy miles away
a TV News report tells Angelica the flood in the graveyard
where her mother is buried is carrying off bodies.

Back at the home screen Bob clicks open some curtains
and a woman appears with open lips, while on Angelica's screen
there's a chapel offering bliss and she moves through it
into an aureole of love dust. Bob clicks off the woman's clothes
one by one and kisses in *excelsis* her screen body: *Oh Angelica!*
Bob and the screen image groan in harmony towards ecstacy.

Angelica in her room, sipping Cola from the machine,
types **BOB** in bold caps and says in a whisper, *Bob, you bastard!*,
then sends out an e-mail to anyone who will listen
asking for pictures of chocolate. On the home screen Bob's search
continues with new vigour into the night's net
punctuated by news from Australia about the cricket.

ELIZABETH GARRETT
VISTA

Standing, with your back turned, taut at work,
Wearing the day's frosted willow-grey skirt
Like a bell of smoke, while a child went on colouring
Under the spell of the Lakeland-Cumberland arc,
You turned suddenly hearing the doorbell ring.
Turned? No – *spun*, till the skirt flared its carillon
And all the poplar leaves of the world shone
Silver, their green gone in the wind's turning.

And here I am, wise at the open door
Trying to remember what it was I came for,
Struck by a knowledge of beauty years beyond
Anything I had yet come to understand,
Watching you disappear down that corridor
Of brilliant sound, my stolen breath in your hand.

ATAR HADARI
LIFE IS VERY LONG

Life is very long. A few mistakes, a few
occasions of some wonder, a few wrongs.
Nothing remains of the day we said goodbye
to the harbour, and I kissed you
on the cheek and you stilled because
you thought someone might be looking.
We stood on the breakwater strand
and faced town and a small figure
came towards us waving his pale hands
and failed completely to take our picture.
You walked all the way back holding your hat
and the whole-earth shampoo bottle
and I promised you a hot bath
if we only could get home before absolute night fell.
And now I do not know if you still care
or how much and I hold discourse
with thin air while out there on the cove
your hat is still pulled and that kiss still burns.

SIMON RAE
CHASER

"What is memory but cutting through smoke?" – Brendan Kennelly

The bar begins to fill with lunchtime regulars.
Veterans of wars and marriages, they bear
their broken blood vessels, expanding
waistlines, thinning scalps and tufty ears

with a stolid survivors' dignity.
They slap their pockets, smokers to a man,
and palm-cupped campfires lift a blue-gray haze
to set a boundary to the afternoon's horizon.

My shout: another Scotch, another pint.
I push my way through a wardrobe of tweed
and twill and catch the barman's eye.
Behind me the Gents door slams unheeded.

I look back to where two stools are drawn
companionably close, willing the skeins of smoke
to form at least the semblance of a ghost.
I know, of course, that you're not going to show

but where's the harm in wishing that you might?
One pint. One Scotch. Many happy returns.
I wave the change away to Cancer Research
and toss your Teachers down my throat. It burns.

DOROTHY NIMMO
A BIRTHDAY PRESENT FOR ROGER JOHN

I would like to send you something very small,
that you could carry with you always, no trouble at all.

I would like to write something you could learn by heart
without even trying and never forget.

I would give you something you already have
that you would keep for the rest of your life, that isn't mine to give.

I would wish you enough time, enough space,
a strong heart, good spirits, a safe place.

But if you turn out to be left-handed, if you suspect your name
may not be your real name,

if you can hear the cry of bats, if you can dowse
for water, if your dreams belong to somebody else,

if, when you stand at the tide's edge looking out to sea
you hear them calling to you, then you must come to me.

MICHAEL HENRY
A GLASS-STOPPERED BOTTLE

Whenever I touch this bottle
summeriness, like dandelions,
rubs off on my fingers;
seeds snowstorm. A glass horseshoe
is brailled into the base
like a coat of arms.

I look through the equator
of its slack yellow transparency,
that stoppered air bubble
or topsy-turvy spirit level
contradicting Galileo,
turning my round world flat.

If I unstoppered it, unbound
the mummy-cloth layers round the neck,
would I fall into dry oblivion
from ether, from chloroform
or simply recoil
from the essence of flowers?

I have taken your instruments
and your way of life to auction.
Were they your one true identity?
A different love this,
lingering on in a half-life
where grainstones of glass jewelesce . . .

I wanted something for nothing,
Murano instead of surgical glass.
To scrape out with a curette
the fruit from the fluid,
to tap on the glass
with obstetric fingers . . .

FRED D'AGUIAR
FROM BILL OF RIGHTS

From Chattanooga, from Brixton (L –, write)
From hallowed be Thy name, Thy kingdom come,
To the Potaro, Essequibo, Demerara,

From 132 gradations – blue-black to chalk-white,
To watch-that-sun-and-overproof-rum,
The sweet potato, bow and arrow warrior,

The near one thousand came and stayed
I am your saviour. Follow me. And we did.
And planted, did we plant, on a hill;

We sang, clapped hands and prayed
For rain, for our cutlass to miss us as we weeded
Before now tending a pot on a window sill;

And the rains came and washed the crops away.
And we planted them again, and they were
Washed away, again; and starved, we starved,

Calling God, Allah, Jah, and Yahweh
Ease this belt tightened to a notch where
None existed, one a hot knife tip carved;

Until the locals took pity on us.
There were, after all, pregnant women,
Children and the very old, in our midst.

They brought wood treated to take this sun,
Zinc as sound as that ship of Nemo's,
And a smile with the force of a blitz.

MATTHEW SWEENEY
SKYLIGHT

When I stand under it
I feel like a fish in winter
looking up through ice.

This defector from a greenhouse,
this window that wandered,
wanting to be neither horizontal nor vertical,
is my favourite. Bay windows,
French windows, portholes – you can keep them.
I don't want to see mountains.
I like *paintings* of waves.

Only the clouds excite me
with their ceaseless messages –
I learned first of the Gulf War
when I read a cloud.
I successfully warned a chef friend
to avoid a consignment of king prawns
that poisoned a rival's clientele.

Sometimes I photograph clouds through glass.

I heard a knocking once, hard,
as on a door, but when I got up there
the visitor was gone.

MATTHEW HOLLIS
WINTERING OUT

for Ian McMillan

If I close my eyes I can picture him
flitting the hedgerow for splints
or a rib of wood to kindle the fire,

or reading the snow for whatever
it was that came out of the trees
and circled the house in the night;

if I listen I can hear him out
in the kitchen, scudding potatoes,
calling the cat in; if I breathe

I can smell the ghost of a fire,
a burning of leaves that would fizz
in the mizzle before snow.

There is in this house now
a stillness of cat fur and boxes,
of photographs, paperbacks, waste-

paper baskets; a lifetime
of things that I've come here
to winter or to burn.

There is in this world one snow fall.
Everything else is just weather.

THE REVIEW PAGES

Burrowing in the Word Hoard

HERMIONE LEE ON A GREAT "MEMORY BANK" AND "LISTENING POST"

The School Bag

Edited by Seamus Heaney and Ted Hughes
Faber, £20 hbk
0 571 17750 6
£12.99 pbk
0 571 17751 4

I STILL HAVE some poetry anthologies from when I was a school in the 1950s and '60s. Palgrave's *The Golden Treasury,* of course, and *A Galaxy of Poems Old and New* (1961), and *Collected Poems (for Secondary Schools)* (1948), and *Poetry for Pleasure* (1942). The editors of these collections addressed their readers as "girls and boys"; they divided the poems into sections called "Love" or "Tales" or (as my *Poetry for Pleasure* had it) "Time, Death and Mutability"; they drew attention to the benefits of reading aloud and "the delight that comes from the remembering and rhythmic chanting of a poem". I found quite a few of the poems from my old school books, and from *The Golden Treasury*, in *The School Bag*: 'The Twa Corbies', 'La Belle Dame Sans Merci', 'Ode to the West Wind', Spenser's 'Prothalamion', Marvell's 'The Garden', Herrick's 'Delight in Disorder', De la Mare's 'The Listeners', Gray's 'Elegy', 'Dover Beach', 'Childe Roland to the Dark Tower Came', Dylan Thomas's 'Fern Hill' (surely the most anthologised poem ever written?), Masefield's 'Cargoes'.

I went in for "rhythmic chanting" as a child, and I'm glad to see that some of the poems I had a passion for saying out loud are here: the scarily tripping measures of 'Up the Airy Mountain', Stevie Smith's gleefully malevolent 'The River God', Hopkin's great mud-stomping walker's song, 'Inversnaid':

What would the world be, once bereft
Of wet and wildness? Let them be left,
O let them be left, wildness and wet;
Long live the weeds and the wilderness yet.

This selection is about traditions ("let them be left"), about memory, and about sound. It is drawing from the two great poet-editors' own memories of their school bags, or "singing schools", and it makes a case for remembering. It is, as Heaney says in his introduction, a "memory bank", which is also "a listening post". Hughes's peculiar "Afterword" gives nothing away about the principles of selection or editorial policy; it just tells you how to memorise poems pleasurably, and how to cultivate an "audial memory", by "listening as widely, deeply and keenly as possible".

This is a serious agenda, and the pleasures of this book are meant to be taken seriously. Heaney introduced their earlier collaborative venture, *The Rattle Bag* (1982) with words like "excitement", "unexpectedness", "chances". This time the appeal, more solemnly, is "to all of us who value poetry and want to remember it, and make sense of their lives". Some of *The Rattle Bag's* choices get in here too, as though there are a few poems that simply can't be done without. These include Blake's 'Auguries of Innocence', Carroll's 'Jabberwocky', Clare's 'The Badger', 'La Belle Dame', Drayton's 'Since there's no help', Tichborne's 'Elegy', Hardy's 'Afterwards', 'Inversnaid', Owen's 'Strange Meeting', and Smart's 'My Cat, Jeoffrey'. From Anon, 'The Twa Corbies', 'Sir Patrick Spens', and sweetly, the 8th century anonymous Irish monk-poet's enchanting praise of his cat Pangur Bán, written in a copy of St Paul's Epistles, and celebrating their mutual tasks of mousing and writing:

So in peace our tasks we ply,
Pangur Bán, my cat, and I;
In our arts we find our bliss,
I have mine and he has his.

But the School Bag's organisation is different and more controlled that *The Rattle Bag's*. There's only one poem allowed by each poet (so the reader can have an interesting time trying to guess what each choice will be). Though there are no section titles, as in my school books, there's a conspicuous arrangement by themes and subjects which merge intriguingly into each other: sea journeys into strange meetings, quests into hauntings, water into winter. There are myths and adventures, animals, workers, famines, tortures, fallings in love, losing love, and "Time, Death and Mutability". The anthology is especially rich in elegies, including a ravishing 18th century Irish woman poet's lament for her dead love Art O'Leary – at the moment my favourite poem in the book:

My love and my dear!
Your stooks are standing,
Your yellow cows milking,
On my heart is such sorrow
That all Munster could not cure it
Nor all the wisdom of the sages.
Till Art O'Leary returns
There will be no end to the grief
That presses down on my heart,
Closed up tight and firm
Like a trunk that is locked
And the key is mislaid.

This old Irish elegy (by Eibhlín Dhubh Ní Chonaill, translated by Eilís Dillon), is typical of the selection. It is rather a dark book, with many poems of pain, ferocity, and raw harshness. Shakespeare is represented, not by sonnets, but by the storm scene from *Lear*, Byron by the Battle of Waterloo in *Childe Harold*, not by 'She Walks in Beauty'. The most savage examples of Anon are in, and one of the few living poets in the book, Anthony Hecht, has a horribly disturbing poem of madness and cruelty, 'Behold the Lilies of the Field'.

Other principles of selection, though not explicit, are evident. The book draws heavily on Scottish poetry and on translations from Irish, Old English, Welsh and classical poetry. (Heaney and Hughes feature only as translators, for instance Heaney of the Irish poet Brian Merrriman, Hughes of *Sir Gawain and the Green Knight*). Though there are poems from America, Canada, and Australasia, there are no African, Indian or European or Eastern European poems at all. (Charlotte Mew is unforgivably absent from both anthologies.) And there are no new voices, very few contemporaries, very little that's modern. You'll look in vain for any of the Motion/Morrison poets from *The Penguin Book of Contemporary British Poetry*, for Les Murray or Peter Porter or Douglas Dunn, or any of the current Irish like Muldoon or Durcan, for any of the great Caribbean voices like Walcott or Brathwaite. Was this because copyright fees were prohibitive, or because the editors felt there was quite enough of this sort of thing already in most people's school bags or curricula? Those twentieth century poets who *are* well known to schoolchildren are represented here by their most archaic examples. So for Larkin we get, not the dry modernity of 'High Windows' or 'Mr Bleaney', but the rhapsodic and antiquarian 'Wedding Wind'; for Lawrence, the dark ancient-feeling myth of 'Bavarian Gentians', not the modern man's dilemma of 'Snake'. There are very few city poems, very little "experimental" poetry. It's a relief to come upon a few of Berryman's savage, funny, furious and utterly contemporaneous *Dream Songs* ("literature bores me, especially great literature") but here he seems like an alien from another poetry-planet.

Though the editors have their greatest fun upsetting chronology, setting Byron next to Gurney or Dickinson next to Dryden, essentially they want to go back, back: to the greatest sounds poetry has made in the past, to the origins of our poetry in ballads and riddles and epic stories. "Because of wine-feast and mead-feast they charged, / Men famed in fighting, heedless of life..." "I was also in Italy with Aelfwine, / Eadwine's son; I have heard that he, / of all mankind, had the quickest hand / at gaining renown in giving out rings / gleaming bracelets, a most generous heart..." "Sad heave where I saw tide ebb, / Rain's drivel that came pouring, / Cold black bed between two slopes, / Salt-filled briny sea-water". There's an awful lot of that sort of thing, very much for the boys, and it makes me want to go off and read Dorothy Parker: "Men seldom make passes / At girls who wear glasses" – unaccountably missing from this selection. But I know really that this word-hoard is worth having, especially when I turn the page and find Herbert's 'The Collar', or the best bits of *In Memoriam,* or Melville's 'The Berg', or 'Lycidas'. This, after all, a book which claims that the art of the human voice is what makes and sustains civilisation. So it begins with Yeats's version of that story in 'The Long Legged Fly', and ends with Dryden's great, scary warning for the end of his century (and ours): "'Tis well an old age is out / and time to begin a new". This is a good book to hold on to, as we set out for the next thousand years of poetry.

Excess Its Own Reward

IAN SANSOM ON THE "WOLFISH PROWESS" OF DON PATERSON

DON PATERSON

God's Gift to Women

Faber, £6.99
ISBN 0 571 17762 X

ON THE INSIDE front page of Don Paterson's first book, *Nil Nil* (1993), is the obligatory short profile of the author: "Don Paterson was born in Dundee, Scotland, in 1963. He left school at sixteen, and since then has worked as a musician, moving to London in 1984. He won an Eric Gregory Award in 1990, and now lives in Brighton". The author profile on the inside front page of Paterson's new book, *God's Gift to Women,* tells us more, with less. It reads: "Don Paterson was born in Dundee in 1963. He works as a musician, and co-leads the jazz-folk ensemble Lammas. He currently divides his time between London and Scotland".

> "Compared to Paterson most other poets read like they're sipping white wine spritzers with an eye on the clock. In the language of contemporary taste and imbibition, if other poets are like the froth on a capuccino, Paterson is a long draw on a four-shot espresso."

Obviously, a lot of things have changed over the past four years. Shares in Scotland have gone up on the literary stockmarket, so it's now assumed that English readers know where to find Dundee. Paterson too has gone up in the world: he no longer merely works as a musician – he now "co-leads" an "ensemble". The publishers also no longer feel that it's necessary to point out to readers that Paterson wins awards: he's proved himself, and so now, appropriately, "divides his time", like all successful writers, rather than merely "living", like the rest of us (though he certainly doesn't do any of this dividing in a sea-side town like Brighton, but rather between London – capital city – and Scotland, a whole nation). The biggest change of all, though, is that we're no longer told that Paterson left school at sixteen.

It's a significant omission, a shrugging off of chips on shoulders ("I'd swing for him, and every other cunt / happy to let my father know his station, / which probably includes yourself. To be blunt",

ran the infamous lines from Paterson's first collection), but in fact we never really needed to be told that Paterson left school at such a sweet and tender age. We can tell. His poetry is so ambitious, so lively, so full of unembarrassed enthusiasm, and at times so brilliant, that it's perfectly clear that he didn't spend two years sweating and stewing over A Levels and then three years stagnating, studying English at university (where, as Les Murray has pointed out, the "real if unadmitted courses might be listed as Caste, Debunking and Alienation").

In *God's Gift to Women* Paterson displays his wit and learning with all the gauc hery and dash typical of the autodidact, belabouring language and ideas, and readers, until they're utterly fed up and exhausted. The front cover of the book shows a still from the film *The Telegrapher's Daughter,* showing a young woman sprawled across a railway line, a steam-train bearing down upon her. Watch out, the image seems to be saying, here I come!

Paterson's *libido ostentandi* derives from an overwhelming desire to impress, and, apparently, initially, from sexual anxiety: "I started writing around '85", he once told an interviewer, "for much the same reason I started playing music, i.e. the rather obscure notion that it might impress women". His wolfish prowess is constantly on display throughout *God's Gift to Women*, sometimes bordering on *braggadocio*, although at the actual moment of bliss in the poem 'from Advice to Young Husbands', the cock becomes a "rapt and silent witness", giving a whole new meaning to Wittgenstein's last gasp in the preface to the *Tractatus*, "whereof one cannot speak thereof one must be silent".

There is usually no such hint of a limit to Paterson's language. The showy, aureate diction of *Nil Nil*, with its smatterings of "mussitates", "columbarium", "zoetrope, "enfilade" and "hieratic", has been replaced in the new book by a more thorough-going use of the dialect and place-names of Scotland, though even Scots might find they need a dictionary to keep up with Paterson's constant impressing and impacting: I had to use the twenty-volume *OED*, second edition, to work out compounds such as "gowk-storm" (presumably a variation on "gowk's-storm", obsolete, from "gowk", "Orig. *Sc.* and *north. dial.*", meaning "1. The cuckoo" and "2. A fool" and thus either "(a) a storm of short duration" or "(b) a spring gale which occurs at the time of the cuckoo's arrival"), not to mention words like "sklent" ("*Sc.* and *north dial.*" again, meaning, "To move, dart, or fall, obliquely; to lie aslant; to give a side-look", or, figuratively, "To deviate from a straightforward course, or from the truth") and "phlebotomist", which I thought at first was maybe a joke – a mock-scholarly reference to one who studies plebs. It's not: a "phlebotomist" is, of course, one who practises *phlebotomy*: "The action or practice of cutting open a vein so as to let blood flow, as a medical or therapeutic operation; venesection, blood-letting, bleeding, hence a blood-letter". Readers may also find that the *Encyclopaedia Britannica* or an *Encarta 96* on CD-ROM comes in handy, for reminders about words like Velocipede (an Anglicised *vélocipède*: "bicycle invented by the Michaux family of Paris in 1862"), and a couple of foreign-language dictionaries wouldn't go amiss either, for looking up some of the fancy loan words, as well as maybe a few guides to world culture, for checking out the foreign names that may have passed you by (who? Oh, *that* Erszébet Szanto!).

There is, then, an exuberance to Paterson's range of language and reference, a daring that is as bold as it can sometimes be bewildering. The undertaker and poet Thomas Lynch, another early school-leaver inordinately proud of his qualifications from the University of Life (or in Lynch's case, one might say, the Polytech of Death), has described a night out on the piss with Paterson: "He still drinks well", writes Lynch, "in a way I never did, allowing excess to be its own reward". Excess its own reward is exactly right. Compared to Paterson most other poets read like they're sipping white wine spritzers with an eye on the clock. Or to put it another way, in the language of contemporary taste and imbibition, if other poets are like the froth on a capuccino, Paterson is a long draw on a four-shot espresso.

The buzz can sometimes produce a headache. Some of the longer poems in *God's Gift to Women* still labour under the dull moon of Muldoon, the reader having to follow winding paths through muddy, half-lit dream territory, and there are a number of other irritations and crackerjack excesses, such as the blank page poem 'On Going to Meet a Zen Master in the Kyushu Mountains and Not Finding Him'. The besetting sin, though, is still Paterson's use of bathos, which is a bad personal habit (in an old interview in *Verse* name-checking Sean O'Brien and talking fancy about poems, Paterson suddenly catches himself on: "I learnt a tremendous amount from Sean; he made me think very hard about things that would never have occurred to me in a million years ... how you can make the poetic voice sound more authoritative through syntax, what happens when you stick the verb at the end of the line, what happens when you mix Guinness, red wine and Kentucky Fried Chicken").

But these are minor complaints. There are at least three wonderful poems in the new collection – 'Candlebird', 'Siesta', and 'A Private Bottling', the rightful winner of the 1994 Arvon Poetry Competition – and at least two good jokes masquerading as poems, 'Postmodern' and 'Homesick Paterson, Live at the Blue Bannock, Thurso' ("but wee man, dye ken, you were the best?"/ "Sorry doll," says I. *"Nae requests"),* which, in the language of the schooling that Paterson long ago abandoned, puts him well above the average.

Ian Sansom is writing a study of W. H. Auden.

For the Duration

by Philip Gross

ANDREW MOTION
Salt Water
Faber, £7.99
ISBN 0 571 19019 7

FOR TWENTY YEARS, Andrew Motion's work has paced along one edge of mainstream poetry, the edge where the voice is so level and quietly spoken that you start to wonder when it will slip into prose. But apart from a couple of novels, his narratives have stayed in verse, where they began. This edge of poetry suggests an East Coast landscape – flat, with low sky and a tinge of melancholy, a feeling of distances, though most of what you see is close at hand. It is a manner made for long walks.

"Further than I usually go..." begins one poem, 'The Clearing', and unspools a single forty-five-line sentence. It does this without signs of strain, following small twists and turns of attention – "just light / collecting and losing its feeble heat, / just mosquitoes dotting my face and hands / with their mad rush of stinging sand" – into associations and reflections and... Full stop. "Who knows, I ask myself. Who knows?" Only in that last line do I see how long the walk has been.

Duration is important in this collection. It seems (though maybe only seems) a world away from creative-writing-class advice to make it terse, and cut, cut, cut. Even a poem which exists for the twist in its tail, like 'Envoy' (lone yachtsman finds Japanese soldier on Pacific island), detains us with two pages of observations wry enough to give the poem the duration it needs, before the pay-off (soldier gets in the yacht and sails away). That is just one poem. 'Sailing To Italy' is a fifty-page account of just that, as Motion follows Keats' last voyage. This memoir perches on the edge of poetry, its prose occasionally freeze-framing into verse, rather as Basho's *Narrow Road To The Deep North* stops to collect itself in haiku: "Imagine everything you know / stops dead. Imagine winds don't blow. / Imagine waves like oily skin..." There are snippets of Keats biography and even a storm, but the nub of the story is an encounter with the sheer tedium of open sea. "Something inside me gives way. I slump at my place in the stern all afternoon, watching the wind run its hand listlessly down the sails, boredom overwhelming me. This is not boredom like before – not a trance. This is real nothing".

'Sailing To Italy' defies the rules of narrative, not building to a climax or a personal revelation. If it grips us, it is through complete attentiveness to detail, both internal and external – a quality gained, it seems, from a willingness to settle in for the duration. There is also the incidental pleasure of its humour. The encounter, above, with "real nothing" suddenly explodes. "Nothing which gouges a hole in my skull and drags out my eyes on stalks to stare into it: failure; despair; disgust curdling into rage. When one of the crew comes up to me I look straight through him. Then he belches vilely and grins: 'Wind'. I want to stick a marlin spike up his arse and throw him to the shark which has just idled past, its fin slick and alert".

Here, duration is faintly Zen. In 'The Spoilt Child' it is a form of cruelty. In a scene quietly charged with the tensions of the English class system we are made to watch through the eyes of a child as his pet Labrador is savaged by a terrier. Worse, because of its matter-of-factness, is the response of the other dog's owner – "a beery man wearing a vest, / and undone, down-trodden shoes, / who carried an all-metal hammer / and a stone he intended to drive through // the bull terrier's teeth to shatter them / if there was no chance of prising them loose, / which he decided at once there wasn't, / giving one, two, three steady blows..." It is the resolute understatement of the poem that stops it being Lawrentian melodrama – that and its duration. The poem takes longer to read than it would have done to happen, and the child never stops noticing the details, one by one. Another poem, 'Hey Nonny', transacts a whole re-evaluation of the world in the moment that it takes a glass to fall.

The quiet voice can be tender, too. 'On The Table' pushes the plain tone to its limits, daring us to find it trivial. "... a dress you have always said / I never told you I liked. Well I did, you know. I did. / I liked it a lot, whether you were inside it or not". Maybe this moment *is* trivial, but Motion gives such an accurate rendering of it, precisely noting the hesitations, sidesteps and assertions and shy jokes of a moment that hangs on someone else's reaction, that the trivial becomes special. Another small transaction at the edge. Read this book slowly; it happens again and again: something prosaic is brought back unexpectedly into poetry.

The Ordinary Privilege of Daylight

by Gillian Allnutt

ELAINE FEINSTEIN

Daylight

Carcanet, £6.95
ISBN 1 85754 291 6

THERE'S A WORD, *farouche*, which doesn't translate easily into English, though my dictionary offers "fierce, wild, savage" and "shy, timid" and "unsociable". The opening poem here, 'Homesickness', is in memory of, and addressed to, Maria Fadeyeva Enzensberger:

> as if I had begun to forget the wildness
> in the gutturals of your laugh

'A Glass of Wine' is "for Emma" and ends

> it is the inner fire still burns in you
> I see and quietly salute:
> indomitable wildness.

'Picnic', written for Roy Tommy Eriksen, recalls an occasion in the Norwegian Arctic and notes:

> His red-haired wife laughs over
> sizzling meat.

And then there's Marina Tsvetaeva, mentioned only once in this collection. I quote again from 'Homesickness': "You were always my Russia: // the voice of Marina's poetry". Elaine Feinstein was the first to set about translating the work of this extraordinary poet into English and Tsvetaeva shadows her own writing yet. Tsvetaeva, in her life and her work, was what I would call *farouche*.

Farouche, I would say, is an aspect of the feminine banished to the shadowlands in most of us and to the dark edges of the daylight celebrated in this collection. 'Bed' depicts the poet with her six-month-old granddaughter, Natasha: "And what I'd wish you to inherit is / ... / the ordinary privilege of daylight". It concludes with this:

> under a cold moon, you may remember
> this bundled duvet as somewhere once
> familiar, where you came to no harm.

We may remember, also, that one of Tsvetaeva's daughters died of starvation in the earlier years of this century.

Many poems in *Daylight* depict and celebrate four generations of family, a long marriage, a host of friends and literary connections, places lived in and visited. They are earthed in an everyday life set always in the history and the global village it is part of. 'Eclipse' describes a family gathering:

> Grandchildren, indulged after the Passover seder,
> have stopped using the mouse on my apple mac
> to stare through the window at the luminous ball
> like primitive people in a world of miracles.

There's a determined attempt, in deference to Richard Dawkins, to materialize the miracle. 'Prayer' says:

> filmy shapes
> that need little more than carbon and water,
>
> evolve like patterns on Dawkins'
> computer, the intricate miracles
> of eye and wing respond to the same
> logic. I accept the evidence.
>
> God is the wish to live. Everywhere

Far stronger, to my mind, are the poems in which – by proxy, by persona – access is gained to the mythology or religion we can no longer allow to shape our being in the world. In 'Fyodor: Three Lyrics' a doctor ("I'm a Swiss doctor, but I read novels") muses on the epilepsy and the Christian faith of Dostoevsky. It may be the need to accommodate the *extremis* of Dostoevsky's own words quoted in the poem – such as "I shall burn everything I once worshipped" – that pulls the pitch, the tone, the rhythm of the language onto a plane other than that of most of the poems in this collection. This happens also in 'Lazarus' Sister':

> All our days
>
> are numbered in a book. I try to imagine
> a way our story can end without a magician.

In spite of my own hankering after anguish / exaltation, I have to assent to the wisdom and warmth of Feinstein's daylight world and her acceptance of human limitation. There's no hubris at all in the way that, again and again, she simply allows the everyday to put out little shoots into infinity.

She has a lovely, unobtrusive way with rhyme it would take whole poems to illustrate. Subtly, in a poem such as 'White Flowers', internal rhyme is used to support, to carry the thread of, narrative or argument through several stanzas. And though the poems read with the ease of prose – I read *Daylight* from cover to cover the minute it arrived and got a lot from that first rushed reading – they are deceptively succinct. With a stressed rather than a metrical line, rhythm works quietly here, calmly laying the poems down line by line. "It was Wordsworth's clear line I wanted", writes Elaine Feinstein in 'Companionship'. She has it.

ELAINE FEINSTEIN
PARADISE

Even the sad music from the car radio is glamorous
this morning, as I take the curve up the hill.
The sun glitters on rainy streets, like
a shoal of herrings in water,
this early March tinges my blood
as yellow touches the strands of a willow.

No-one knows where I am. No-one
cares what I do. It's alarming
to be untethered as a kite slipped from
a child's hand, and then blown past
this high street of shop windows: Monsoon,
French Connection, Waterstone's.

The last gives me pause. I wonder
whether it was cowardice or duty
denied me this freedom so long,
to take comfort from the name on a book spine,
or italic under a photo, while the blood
of my life found a pulse only in song.

THE CLASSIC POEM

SELECTED BY JENNY JOSEPH

RUTH PITTER WAS a poet devoted from childhood to the craft. Her work exemplifies an expert handling of a range of forms, that of 'In the open' being one of those she was best at.

In her introduction to the 1968 Macmillan edition of her *Collected Poems* she wrote "My purpose has never varied. It has been simply to capture and express some of the secret meanings which haunt life and language: the silent music, the dance in stillness, the hints and echoes and messages of which everything is full..."

Her poetry and her loves were not ethereal but of the earth earthy. For her a "real poem...begins and ends in mystery...that secret movement of the poet's being in response to the secret dynamism of life". It is also a "structure...clothed in the legal tender and common currency of language; perhaps the simpler the better", so "the crowning wonder, if it comes, may emerge clear of hocus-pocus".

I don't think this poem needs any advocacy from me. Once before your eyes or in your ears you will understand why I have chosen it, but here are some "reasons".

I find pleasing the movement of the words across the rhyme and verse scheme, the sentences like threads in strong weave running across a firm base. After the opening imperative it is all one sentence till the end of the second verse. The rhymes get enough emphasis without being intrusive because they are not end stopped. In each verse there are slight but pivotal differences of structure, all so that exactly the right amount of weight comes on each right word. The one exception to the full rhyme is the haunting half-rhyme in the last verse (the only weak rhyme in a poem where nearly all the words are monosyllables).

Every time I read the poem I find more subtlety and variety contributing to its singleness and centrality. If you will read it, perhaps aloud, just paying attention to the punctuation, I think you will hear what I do in this perfectly "right" poem.

Jenny Joseph's *Selected Poems* (including 'Warning'), are published by Bloodaxe.

RUTH PITTER
IN THE OPEN

Move into the clear.
Keep still, take your stand
Out in the place of fear
On the bare sand;

Where you have never been,
Where the small heart is chilled;
Where a small thing is seen,
And can be killed.

Under the open day,
So weak and so appalled,
Look up and try to say,
Here I am, for you called.

You must haunt the thin cover
By that awful place,
Till you can get it over
And look up into that face.

Ruth Pitter (1897–1992) was awarded the Queen's Gold Medal for Poetry in 1955. Her *Collected Poems*, introduced by Elizabeth Jennings, are published by Enitharmon Press.

The Oxford Master

SEAN O'BRIEN ON THE VIRTUOSITY OF JOHN FULLER

JOHN FULLER

Collected Poems

Chatto, £20

ISBN 0 7011 6612 6

IN THE OPENING section – 1954–65 – of John Fuller's *Collected Poems* there are several examples of kinds of poem which might be thought more nearly contemporary than those dates imply. There is the ur-Martianism of 'Flood Box':

> Imagined depth! Within its grip
> White figures struggle to be free.
> Above, the motorboats unzip
> Their tinted wrinkled scenery
> And breakers fall like piano lids,
> Unloosing liquid horrors: black
> Regency-hair crabs, snotty squids
> And cherub penises of wrack.

The ingenious eye associated with the early Craig Raine is subjected to a brisker, more formal regime than Raine's, the perceptions ticked off on a clipboard as the poem gets on with the work of eventually undermining (or submerging) the mastery it appears to be displaying. The stylishness is both an enjoyable performance and a means of disclosing the very uncertainties it masks. Every facet of the poem can be said to be in play; a perceptual *tour de force* becomes dramatic.

Nearby is 'Pictures From a '48 De Soto', where further devices which have now become more commonplace are examined:

> Humped in this swart sedan, paper half-lowered,
> The automatic at my side snug as a cancer,
> I watch the house. Or in the house myself
>
> Look at my wrist, insane with jealousy...

There is the incorporation of genre material – the Chandleresque tableau – and the treatment of the narrative voice as an identity made of successive shots ("Black opening mouth, the sound switched off"), so that it becomes an object to be considered among others in the poem. There is a sense that the whole thing is a performance, a shadowplay, but equally a feeling that it is only through artifice that the poem can live. There is the withholding of information and thus of perspective. There is the toneless depiction of the grotesque, the conversion of violence into image ("palms thud wildly on / The glass") and a refusal to resolve the story:

> Dwarfs wrestle behind glass. Dresses
> Are cut to the buttocks' cleft. Half-shaved men
> Are running sheeted through the empty square.

A few pages away is 'The Ballad of Lord Timbal', the tale of a rich and futile young man seeing off his guests at the end of their stay before taking to his yacht and meeting his death:

> He sailed into a mid-sea storm
> And there without a sound
> The swollen sails exploded
> And Lord Timbal was drowned.

It is perhaps in Auden that Fuller has learned (as he has learned much else) how to direct a ballad between the seemingly indifferent voice of time and the eyeblink of detail which makes events intimate – "His servant drove ten hampers down, / Bursting with carp and hock, / And the train was out and the party gone / Like a glimpse of a summer frock". 'Lord Timbal' is a moral tale of a bleak sort, but it earns its final freezing blast by reproducing the abruptness and near non-sequitur found in some traditional ballads:

> His body was slowly borne along
> On the stretchers of the sea,
> And all the drums of the Spanish coast
> Beat in sympathy.

The list could be extended to include the strange sonnets, the slow motion narrative 'Girl With a Coffee Tray', the Angela-Carter-ish 'In a Railway Compartment', the bizarre *paysages moralisés* of the slightly later work, and the continuous sense that Fuller's clipped accuracy and formal brio are means of signalling a deeply felt perplexity about the relationship between the peremptory facts of desire and death and the poet's shining instruments. But the conclusion seems clear: if there is English postmodernism, Fuller's work is one of its starting-points. It might be fair to add that if Fuller, as is sometimes said, has fostered a line of poets, the real fulfilment of his work is to be found in the handful of major poems written by James Fenton, his friend and sometime collaborator. Fenton's 'A Staffordshire Murderer', 'A German Requiem', 'A Vacant Possession', 'Nest of Vampires' and the early 'The Pitt-Rivers Museum' all benefit greatly from the curiosity about the poem's frame of reference and the nature of its authority which are present from Fuller's earliest work. The difference between the two poets is at first light-heartedly set out in Fuller's 'Letter To James Fenton', where Fuller considers the inclinations of the poet: "Poets hate to have directives: / They're on their own, not on collectives..." Bowing to Fenton's political urgency in his Marxist days, in an Audenesque ending Fuller tries to square the circle of art and life:

Meanwhile we have to try to bring
Some order to that circus ring
Where people feel and think and sing.
    For at its centre
There's no escape from anything
    And we must enter.

Yet it has been Fenton who has attempted to write history. While Fuller offers a summary of liberal and personal doubt – "The world is all that is the case. / You cannot see it if you are inside it" –

Fenton has seen the world as an historical process, an enclosure mapped with an Amazon of ideological fissures. If Fuller has spent his career charting a high plateau, Fenton has encountered a few spectacularly forbidding and insistent mountains. Of course, it will not do simply to use one poet to damn the other: even the most suspicious critic is likely to be drawn back to the habitual brilliance of Fuller's technique, allied as it is with an imagination that begins where most others would leave off. In recent years Fuller's work has taken on a fresh urgency, in poems such as 'The Mechanical Body', or the fluent complexities of 'England':

At the heart of England we listen to old stories
With an amusement that guarantees their lack of any
                                                    power
To direct our attention to what they may be saying
    And off we solidly stump
Past the gingerbread cathedral and the factory blur
    To the scenery we prefer.

The pertinence of this reading of the role of illusion in nationhood (history is what you have so that you can ignore it) seems particularly evident at the moment. The poem also invites us to remember that place is "never / The involving predicate that something meant, / Simply an accident". Instance, epigram and strangeness combined: disagree as some of them might with Fuller's quietism, poets of the younger generations will have their work cut out to match him. It's good to record that Chatto's production of this book appropriately reflects its importance. It's solid, on decent paper, clearly printed.

Dark-Land

by John Burnside

GEOFFREY HILL

Canaan

Penguin, £7.99
ISBN 0 14 058786 1

IN A RECENT interview, Peter Porter remarked upon the stand-up tendency in recent British poetry:

"One of the great problems of the 20th century has been that poets, recognising that there's a lack of seriousness in the world, have turned themselves to a certain degree into stand-up comedians... I think we are all of us tarred with that brush to a certain extent, because we do want to hear laughter in the hall, we do want to be loved by our audiences" (*Verse*, Volume 13, Nos 2 & 3). He then goes on to talk about the one poet who seems prepared to risk being serious – seeming dull, even – for the sake of his work. That poet is Geoffrey Hill.

It is true that the fear of being, or seeming dull, of not being liked, haunts artists in every discipline at the present time. Perhaps it was always so. Better the easy laugh, or the prescribed response, than blank looks and a mystified silence. It takes courage – or perhaps indifference – to pursue the difficult path, where few, in the age of the three-minute attention span, are prepared to follow. With *Canaan*, Geoffrey Hill renews, once again, his commitment to that path.

The subject matter of the book is, as is so often the case in Hill's work, the land of England: what was once the New Jerusalem, and is now Bunyan's "Dark-Land". Hill has always concerned himself with the relationships between history and the present moment, sometimes fusing the two in rich and delicate myths, as in *Mercian Hymns*, or 'An Apology for the Revival of Christian Architecture in England'. His engagement has been with a continuity of values, with concepts of justice and order, as they are conveyed and perpetuated within a tradition. As he has said, in an interview with John Haffenden, "I think there's a real sense in which every fine and moving poem bears witness to this lost kingdom of innocence and original justice. In handling the English language the poet makes an act of recognition that etymology is history. The history of the creation and debasement of words is a paradigm for the loss of the kingdom of innocence and original justice".

Yet, whereas in his earlier poetry there are flashes of dark wit, (particularly, as Porter notes, in *Mercian Hymns*), *Canaan* is the work of a saddened and angry writer: the book wavers between jeremiad and simple elegy, expressing cold rage, on the one hand, at the corruption of Parliament, with its "masters of servile counsel" and "grandees risen from scavenge"; lamenting, on the other, the England of Blake, Bunyan, Churchill, Constable, Elgar, Law, Marvell, Milton, Pugin, Ruskin, Wesley – a legendary England, to whose vigorous intellectual and moral values it once seemed appro-

priate to aspire.

In *Canaan*, Hill acknowledges that such values are a thing of the past. He sees an England that is, "now of genius / the eidolon", and, aware of his own outmoded stance, he notes, in passing, "Perhaps I too am a shade". It is the time of stand-up comedians and self-serving politicians; the central notions which recur here again and again – probity, justice, equity – are out of fashion. All that remains in these poems is to describe the present state of affairs and to work out, however tentatively, an honest way of proceeding.

Answers do not come easily. In 'Parentalia', however, with its epigraph from the book of Daniel – "And he said, Go thy way, Daniel: for the words are closed up and sealed till the time of the end" – some first steps are taken:

> But go, as instrumental, of
> the Lord, life-bound to his
> foreknowledge
> and in his absence making
> your return
> to the generations, the
> rosaceae,
> the things of earth snagging
> the things of grace,
> darkened hawthorn, its late
> flare, that stands
> illustrious
>
> ('Parentalia')

This advice – from God to Daniel, from the poet to his readers – stands at the centre of the collection. In *Canaan*, Hill pursues the finest English tradition – that of dissent; at the same time, he feels his obligation to innocence and original justice, and the true work of the poem, which cannot be all lament, or elegy:

> Go your ways, as if in thanksgiving:
>
> ('Parentalia').

Notice that "as if". There are few laughs in *Canaan*; it is not a book that will please the stand-up comedians. For this reason alone, it commands respect.

Poet in Comfortable Sandals?

by Jane Holland

Sappho through English Poetry

Edited by Peter Jay and Caroline Lewis
Anvil, £7.95
ISBN 0 85646 273 X

IT IS NOTHING short of a Greek tragedy that only fragments of Sappho's nine volumes of poetry have survived antiquity. Since her infamous love-sick suicide, myth and supposition have dogged this poet from Lesbos, in spite of her reputation as one of the greatest poets of all time. Many past male translators attempted to conceal the fact that her love poems were aimed at women, with most of her female admirers (generally unschooled in Greek) none the wiser. This cover-up might have succeeded, if times had not grown more liberal and translations correspondingly more literal. Unfortunately, their efforts drew more attention to her sexuality than her talent, and Sappho unjustly emerged as the shadowy forerunner of today's lesbian feminist writer: in other words, a poet in comfortable sandals.

This Anvil edition selects different versions and evocations of Sappho from Catullus to Michael Longley, concentrating on her best-known poems (mainly ' Ode to Aphrodite' and 'That man sitting opposite you', which are among the longest pieces found intact). The chronological arrangement provides a fascinating and often highly amusing insight into how each age has approached this poet, but its narrow focus makes this more of a companion volume than a definitive work. In their excellent Introduction, editors Peter Jay and Caroline Lewis admit to this deficiency, but hope that "the pleasure of comparison of different approaches to the same important poems makes up for this", and I think that attitude is partially justified. Certainly this edition would make a perfect introduction to Sappho for readers who might otherwise be baffled by a straightforward translation of her collected fragments.

What is significant is how many translators have failed to capture the very "Sapphic spirit" which one assumes inspired them in the first place. But just as a landscape may change drastically according to its inhabitants, so Sappho seems to have been recast in the image of each successive society. Accordingly, the simple style and clear voice of the original Greek is often lost under the weight of "fashionable" poetic devices, although as the versions move closer to our own times there is a return, not surprisingly, to a plainer style. Compare these two versions of the same poem, the first from E. Burnaby Greene (d. 1788):

> Happy the youth, who free from care
> Is seated by the lovely Fair!
> Not Gods his ecstasy can reach,
> Who hears the music of thy speech;
> Who views entranc'd the dimpled grace,
> The smiling sweetness of thy face

and this from Robert Lowell (1917–1977):

> I set that man above the gods and heroes –
> all day, he sits before you face to face,
> like a cardplayer. Your elbow brushes his elbow –
> if you should speak, he hears.

Both translations stray quite cheerfully from the original, but Lowell's attempt is closer to Sappho's, not only in terms of a stricter adherence to her stanza form and pattern of caesuras, but also by his unelaborate language. If anything, it is rather too flat (apart from the fanciful "cardplayer" image) to convey the almost physical tension that runs below Sappho's lines. But each version must speak for its own time, and perhaps it is only to be expected that Sappho's unique style would be inimitable.

What this collection achieves is a commentary on our own literary history, rather than simply a nod to a great classical poet. Since the editors have concentrated more on versions written before the first half of this century, only a few women writers are represented here, but those that are contribute some revealing versions. Inspired by tales of Sappho's unrequited love, Katherine Bradley and Edith Cooper (writing collectively as Michael Field in 1889), provide me with a suitably controversial parting shot in their poem 'Why are women silent?':

> ...women can attain
> The great measures of the masters only if they love
>   in vain.

The Great All-Rounder

by Ruth Padel

HOMER

The Odyssey

Translated by Robert Fagles,
Viking, £25
ISBN 0 670 82162 4

OUR IDEAS OF ourselves and of poetry would be quite different if the *Odyssey* had got lost in some Dark Age. It shaped Western ideas of how poems present selves. The man trying to get home, losing companions, working with grown-up son to get rid of thugs; re-finding wife and dad; powerful when he's lost everything except the resources of his own mind and body; inventive, compassionate, good at lies, but never losing integrity: Odysseus is the great all-rounder. A man women want, who's never blown off-course by them. We're talking male identity: the Greek-cum-Hollywood ideal. For all time, this poem sexually politicized the idea of life as a journey into knowledge which is also a homecoming.

It did it in wonderful language: sensuous, direct, formulaic, quick, full of images, intensely interested in physical detail. (Dirty washing; the smell of a belch.) In the *Iliad*, physical domesticity comes over mainly in similes, tragic counterpoint to the battlefield. Men fight over corpses like flies round milking-pails. In the *Odyssey*, the physicality of the similes is closer to that of the action. Danger is everywhere, domestic interiors included. The theory that the *Odyssey* was composed by a woman expressed reaction to its lighter, more homogeneous feel.

This makes it harder to translate. The bronze primitivism that crackles through Logue's *Iliad* is risky here. You want translations for different things: you'll want Fagles for directness plus a vivid sense of the physical. Like Odysseus getting recognized by his dog:

Infested with ticks, half-dead from neglect,
here lay the hound, old Argos.
But the moment he sensed Odysseus standing by

he thumped his tail, nuzzling low, and his ears
                                        dropped,
though he had no strength to drag himself an inch
toward his master. Odysseus glanced to the side
and flicked away a tear, hiding it from Eumaeus,
diverting his friend in a hasty, offhand way:
"Strange, Eumaeus, look, a dog like this,
lying here on a dung-hill..."

This has all of Fagles' virtues. Internal rhyme holding lines together; plainness; informality alongside the stiffness that goes with formulas like "long-enduring Odysseus".

Similes? When Odysseus reaches land after days in the sea, he cuddles under tree-roots:

A fine litter of dead leaves had drifted in,
enough to cover two men over, even three,
in the wildest kind of winter known to man.
Long-enduring Odysseus, over-joyed at the sight,
bedded down in the midst and heaped the leaves
                                        around him.

Emotion is buried in the plain language as the hero's body-heat is buried in dry leaves. The Boys' Own adventure parts are equally page-turning.

The area I'm uneasy with is direct speech. Fagles tries to get in all tonalities. It doesn't always work. Hermes, telling Calypso to release Odysseus, says,

steer clear of the rage of Zeus!
Or down the years he'll fume and make your life a
                                        hell.

"Fuming" gets done in traffic jams. It is not what kings of gods do when disobeyed. I know Fagles is trying for the colloquial but it sounds bathetic. (So does "make your life a hell".) But the speech is often lovely, like Penelope listening to Odysseus' reaction to her bed-moving suggestion:

"*Odysseus*! Don't flare up at me now, not you,
always the most understanding man alive!
The gods, it was the gods who sent us sorrow –
they grudged us both a life in each other's arms
from the heady zest of youth to the stoop of old age!

I'm uneasy about "heady zest of youth", but the repetitions and rhythm get the emotion beautifully. In all, a direct, musically thoughtful, and sensitive translation.

The Terza Rima Tightrope

by Steve Ellis

DANTE

The Divine Comedy

Translated Peter Dale

Anvil, £25

ISBN 0 85646 287 X

IN JUDGING A translation of Dante it is not the success (or failure) of a particular episode that first counts, but the sustained readability of the whole. Attention has always been focused on *The Divine Comedy*'s dramatic highlights, and any translation that can encourage the reader through the absorbing passages of exposition, description and even allegory, as Peter Dale's does, deserves gratitude. But readers have to give the translator time to educate them into the style and voice used; to dip straight into Ugolino or Brunetto Latini is to court inevitable disappointment. Thus to over-react to the very opening (especially in the light of Mandelstam's comment on the bookjacket about "wrestling Dante from the grip of schoolroom rhetoric") would be a mistake:

> Along the journey of our life half way,
> I found myself again in a dark wood
> Wherein the straight road no longer lay.

The inversion of word order in the first line, the dreary "wherein" in line 3, might promise another victory for schoolroom rhetoric, but in fact Dale generally manages to avoid such features, especially in the opening cantos. He notes in the Introduction how he aimed for a version "that could be read naturally without having to stop to puzzle over the word order or diction, without being distracted by awkward and archaic rhymes", and how his own *terza rima* attempts to reproduce the "fluency and impetus" of Dante's. Certainly a natural word order and a modern diction are impressively sustained, but the problem of rhyme is more intractable. The translation is subtitled *A Terza Rima Version*, and what is obviously Peter Dale's central concern is likely to become the reader's too.

In a translation of some 14000 lines the *terza rima* is sustained better than anyone has a right to expect, but it does remain a constant distraction, even when going well; when not going well it's like watching a tightrope-walker being buffeted by high winds. Take the opening of *Hell* proper, and Dante's reaction to the inscription above the entrance in canto 3:

> These words, in colour dark, the entablature
> Above a portal showed. "Master", said I,
> "Fearful, I feel, the sense that they adjure".

Here the fluency is offset by redundancies occasioned by the rhyme. "Entablature" is a lovely word in this position, but in meeting with it one already feels a dread about how it will be matched, and sure enough line 3, ending in "adjure", is a desperate rendering of Dante's crisp "*Maestro, il senso lor m'è duro*". There are enough blemishes of this kind to keep the reader nervous, and the blunders in this translation nearly all come in the line-endings: the old tailor squints at the needle's *shank* (rather than eye) in canto 15, and Brunetto's phrase on seeing Dante is the implausible "Why, this is wonder at the height!" (the rhyme-word is "sight"); the feverish of *Hell* 30 are steaming "like hands washed by wintry banks", which adds a riverside location for the ablution which is not immediately perspicuous and also not in Dante, and so on.

It would be churlish to multiply instances when the *terza rima* is handled for the most part very effectively, but this is the translation's characteristic defect. It is most telling in the passages of impassioned dialogue: Brunetto's greeting above is the outburst "*Qual maraviglia!*" in Italian. Dale's verse works well in the more formal passages where the pentameter comes into its own: the description of the pageant in the earthly paradise for example. *Terza rima* in Italian is facilitated not only by the number of rhyming words but by the liquidity of the language and a bouncing vowel-driven rhythm; English *terza rima* in iambic pentameter in many parts replaces Dante's sensitivity to the speaking voice with obtrusive formality, however "natural" the diction. This translation is indeed a monument of meticulous versification; but what Dale terms the "freshness" of Dante – the meadow, moorland and mountain of his style – has been converted into an acreage of cultivated English lawn, not free from molehills. One admires the artistry and patient tending; one sighs for the open road.

JOHN GOODBY
ONE OF THE PTOLEMYS

Twelve pianos were flinging "La Violette"
upstairs and down. Our guide, Sister Two-Eight,
smiled her saint's smile. Do Ursulines flagellate?
Use hairshirts? Oubliettes? I'd read Diderot,
I shivered in the sun in their kitchen-garden.
(And how do they move? On *castors*?) Be Magdalens,
I say, before you kneel at that wicket – sheeted
furniture of heaven, Suttee-hearts immolated!

Queasy, I left for God's air, the river strolling
by freely, at a man's pace. The dollies
were keening Higos in the typhus holds
of transports; shawlies and stumpy doodeens
idled on Patrick's Bridge. In their cabins
they'll lie in bed all day "for the hunger".
(*I'd* go without on Friday, with its four fish –
fish fried, fish raw, fish stinking and ling!)

The Coal Quay shows they'd rather die than pray
or stuff County stirabout – scarecrow-gear,
stalkoes crying hoops, bottles, nails. Ignore
scenery or art; the Sublime of Want
sells Croker's *Tours* and Lover's *Character.*
They starve a stone's-throw from the scuffed array
of the Mardyke; all gloom, but for a red butcher
calling us back to buy some "honest meat".

The "tyrant sister kingdom", then? Yet laws
didn't spoil the Art School for want of a brush,
or cobweb the libraries of a book-crazed town,
or leave temples unporticoed. It's as much
the *braggadocio* starts, indolent trailings off
*   *   *   *   *

Palmyra's sadness, Thebes-gated thistle-fields,
walls fissile with hart's-tongue and maidenhair.

Laugh or cry? The street arabs' talk may range
to *one of the Ptolemys*! – yet saw-millers
were milling at the vitriol-flingers trial
as we galloped out; a place without change
for a five pound note, like our fire that sulked
until Peggy brought up coals – in a CHINA PLATE!
(its coal-dusted head the Queen's, or my wife's,
still bonneted, bobbing in the packet's wake).

MARTYN CRUCEFIX
THESE STRANGERS

We do not have it yet,
but we two are the real bad news
to be put back
like broken toys into a room
with the other first-glimpsers

the first-portraits-
of-our-fruitfulness,
the oh-what-perfect-tiny-hands,
delighters in a snub-nose,
the eye-pit lookers-on

– now, we are the grotesques

flimsy as cartoons, folding ourselves
into bolted chairs, each
stricken with a molten storm
overhead, monstrous,
specific and as fearful
of scaring these strangers
as of the news we do not have

since they have already
glimpsed it, begun to guess
why we do not move off
as we should and their looks
accuse us, say we have betrayed
every last imagined, petted ounce.

EDWIN MORGAN
RED DEER

We are the deer
and we are here.
We like it here.
We couple and we fight,
eat everything in sight,
and some say that's not right.
We're nearly half a million strong:
suppose we ran in unison,
gliding like a spreading stain
across the windy high terrain,
who could cull us, who could kill us,
smell of stalkers couldn't chill us.
– That's a dream we sometimes dream
beside the falls and roaring stream,
and then we wake to rifle-cracks
and feel the kitchen at our backs.
Brothers, get those antlers clashing!
Bellow if the rain is lashing!
Sisters, trot through bog and heather,
take dainty fill of every weather!
Ears cocked, nostrils flared,
browse and watch, don't be scared.
Watch and browse, green delight,
shoots and roots, soon comes night,
soon comes snow
when you must go
starving and gaunt
downhill to haunt
the homes of men.
What then, what then?

GRETA STODDART
ALLIES

I first realised you were not who I'd taken you to be
when I found you sleeping in the middle of a dark afternoon.
Sent home early, ashamed, in tears, I wandered
round the empty house and shambled into your room.
The curtains fell like a shroud around your bed,
around you who never slept, whose job it was to watch over me
but who now lay stirring your own dreams, elsewhere, insouciant.
Then you opened your eyes, you must've felt my breath,
and looked at me like a patient coming to, resenting
the first face she sees after a deep and bewildering absence.

The second time was when your mother died. You lost
your tongue and roamed the house, opening doors,
seeing us, your children, neither here nor there but somewhere
as tiny figures receding into unimportant corners.
We held your life now, in our, smaller, hands,
and we could no longer touch you, without thinking first.
You spent the night turning her habits into yours;
putting silk you'd never wear to sleep in drawers,
collecting foreign coins your husband forgot to spend,
perfuming the rooms with leaves that took years to die.

And the third time, when we were all sent home early.
I didn't know that room had a door 'til I saw it shut.
The house had tried to seal itself against us,
and even the dog bristled, but my brother, idiot,
never one to listen, listened at the door then pushed.
I was curious that you came out fully clothed and so quickly,
proud that all you did was zip up your thigh,
flick your hair, look flushed and embarrassingly young.
My sisters stared at the ground, doomed. But me,
I like to think I looked you straight in the eye.

DAVID WHEATLEY
ALBA

the river stuttering over its weirs to the bay
a heron sleeping erect in the shallows, a hook-necked
swan treading the grey-black ferment of the tide
the pronged moon and a few weak stars overhead
and the papers in bundles outside shops and the shutters going up —

It's getting light. Light on the water and light in the streets:
an ecliptic sliver of gold along the cathedral's
cupola, the raindrops on the hedgerow leaves
seeded with light like amphibians' eyes.
The first train's whistle carries half-choked on the wind
from the station I'm walking towards and will reach
in good time to sit and watch the commuters descend on,
briefcases in hand and clutching their papers like scrolls,
from a second-class carriage. I'm running ahead of time
on nameless streets, an unopened umbrella
crooked on my arm or cheekily dragged along railings,
an aimless wire-haired mongrel jog-trotting
for a few hundred yards beside me, tail in the air,
then turning back as unpredictably as it arrived.

It's getting light. I look for the moment of secret convergence
of colour and blackness before day prevails,
the exact shade of its motionless doubt before birth,
like knowing a face and not being able
to give it a name, like catching a breath,
like the sound of a voice or the sound of a silence
hesitating between "yes" and "no".
I match the deckle-edged skyline I'm watching fade up
to all I remember, and match a vague mood of desire
to what I can only imagine the city containing:
raindrops shaken from the hedgerows falling
over your face and into my hand on your face
in a garden where the birds peck at the winter earth
and find nothing, and a cat in the flower-bed arches
its spine to leap and does not, a heron standing
on one leg under a beech tree in full
November disarray, curtains flapping loose
in an open window while I run barefoot over the lawn,
my fingers covered in earth; all in daydream;
and however I try to connect

the water I hear running in mains-pipes under
the streets I walk with the raindrops that I imagine
falling over your face and into my hand
I fail.

I tell myself it will have got light
in the pupils of your opening eyes, but in
your irises there is always room for sleep.
The dreams we will rise from tomorrow have started already,
threading their clew through labyrinths with no more
possible end than there is an end to the wrong
turns open to me whether I stay or go any further.
You too think you are free and move in a maze
however you try to believe the paths that led
you here were of your own choosing, or that you
are rooted any more deeply than the shadows
that climbed your bedroom wall as you slept.
There is only the dark and the light coming on.
Cats sit on doorsteps and wait to be fed, the newspapers
wait to keep their appointments over breakfast
with eyes still dull from the sleep they will hardly dislodge
and this is the day —

the hiss of a cigarette butt dropped in a platform puddle
newsprint on my fingers numb with the chill
coffee the colour of rust in a Styrofoam cup
the sound of the leaving train's whistle and under it
the wind that sooner or later will have to blow over.

PAUL FARLEY
"THE IGLOO"

The re-name was partly brewery-inspired
and wholly apt. Two anoraks
fought in the snow – closed-circut slapstick,
sliding about on their arses, until
one pulled a knife. It's as far as *Crimewatch* could show.

The femoral blood thawed away
but the place stayed tainted somehow, despite
fairy-lights and a time-bending Happy Hour
that lasted three. Custom slacked:
on Boxing Night, Time was called to an empty bar.

I walked past it twice every day –
its dry urinals spiked with pineapple cubes;
its chairs stood on tables for months on end
praying for amnesia, for second chances;
its old name, dated in local stone,
carved out of reach of design consultants.

It re-opened in spring. A fruit machine
blinked awake as if nothing had happened.
But the small print over the lintel has changed;
the cancer appeal jeroboam vanished.

A coat of brilliant white covers doors, sills, frames
and the dancefloor shines like a rink.
A nice touch – faces under ice look up skirts
and a photograph of the North Pole fills a wall:

winter has come indoors to keep warm.

ANTHONY THWAITE
PSALMODICS

These old arcane contritions, ancient sounds
Compounded of such alien traditions –
Shinto, Judaic, Syriac, Hindu – thread
Beseeching wails with solemn ululations
Over the holy places, over the buried dead.
Canticle, veda, sutra, chant their still
Archaic keening among the killing grounds,
The darkness into which their pure sounds spill.

Something to do with love, with grief, with death,
All share this common melody, ascend
And fall and rise again, repeat again
Cadences that return, that never end
Until the melisma of extended pain
Shudders and drops its wordless stubborn stress
With resignation, with exhausted breath,
Over the risen hope, over the hopelessness.

MICHAEL LONGLEY
ELEGY
in memory of George Mackay Brown

After thirty years I remember the rusty scythe
That summarised in the thatch the deserted village,

And the anchor painted silver so that between showers
Between Hoy and Stromness it reflected the sunshine.

Now the anchor catches the light on the ocean floor.
The scythe too is gleaming in some underwater room.

MARTIN REED
DERBYSHIRE, 1995

Pigeons circle the town and tumble down
Through bonfire smoke and mist to settle in
Their corrugated lofts among the sprouts
And bicycles, the bamboo wigwams
Hung with runners, blackened by the frost.
The land is hollowed out so houses sometimes
Lean and gardens sag. We've lived enough
To see the place drained of its mystery
But we've forgotten nothing. Like those voices
Heard in sculleries and living-rooms,
So real they brought the grieving families in
To recognise a husband or a son.
The search was long abandoned and the town
Was settling, bright with rose bay willow herb.
Officials came and listened to the wind
Through chimneys, mice in the walls. What did they know?
Men had walked up from the ground while teams
Searched miles away, men given up for dead.
In blinded tunnelings we knew their words
But we were powerless, and they still call from
Winding-houses spinning in the shifts
Of steam and steel. The coughing shaft spools out
Its aching limbs that haul themselves to daylight's
Cool, white sheets where love and silence waits.
We know all this. It happens well below
The surface and there's nothing ever said.

SINÉAD MORRISSEY
FEBRUARY

There is no kindness in me here. I ache to be kind, but the weather
Makes me worse. I burrow and snear. I stay small, low, cheap, squander

All signs of the thaw by screwing my eyes. It's easier in the dark.
Defeat is the colour of morning, the grey that engenders the honeymoon flats

And the chess-board of rice-fields between this block and that.
Each field is marked

For the administering of cement, this month or the next.
I am living in boom, before the door-frames are in or the drive-ways drawn.

The new exit from the station to the South
Makes Nagoya spread, calls it out further than one city's insatiable mouth

Could dream. Factories chew through a mountain beyond my window
And each time I look at it it's less. In the world before the war

This place was famous: a stopping-house for the tired and sore.
There was one road only in Japan, and all who walked it walked

Through this town. There are photographs of women in an amber light,
Stopped dead in their surprise at being captured as the image of a time.

Behind them all, the mountain rises white.
They say it stayed so all winter long, a shut door to the North.

The snow scatters now without it. When all the fields are town,
The mountain, stones, it will be Spring, and I'll be called on

To be generous. There will be days when fruit-trees, like veterans
Left standing here and there in pools of shade, will forget about use and bloom.

The Great Precursor

HARRY CLIFTON ON THE LAUREATE OF THE AGE OF ANXIETY

W. H. AUDEN

Prose 1926–1938

Faber, £40
ISBN 0 571 17889 5

In Solitude for Company:
W. H. Auden after 1940

Edited by Katherine Bucknell and Nicholas Jenkins
Oxford University Press
ISBN 0 19 818294 5

STAN SMITH

Writers and their Work: W. H. Auden

Northcote House / British Council, £7.99
ISBN 0 7463 0736 5

BARRING SOMETHING EXTRAORDINARY in the coming three years, this century can be said, for better or worse, to have its poetry now. In the case of Auden the jury is still out, but a remark made by his friend Cecil Day Lewis in the *Irish Times* two decades ago, to the effect that Eliot would be no more than a footnote to twentieth-century English poetry while Auden would be a giant, begs again the question of his present place in the pantheon.

Prose 1926–1938, the first in the prose volumes of the *Complete Works*, is not perhaps the best place to start a reassessment, which is not to suggest that it isn't a marvellous read. It is just that substantial parts of it are not written by Auden at all, and the collaborations with Louis MacNeice in *Letters From Iceland* and Christopher Isherwood in *Journey To A War* do not often show him to his best advantage. Another collaboration included here, with T. C. Worsley on the theory of education, is fascinating mainly for what it shows of the range of involvement a bossy, socially confident poet like Auden could get away with in the 'thirties. And that is not to mention the inevitable Spain, on which one rather stilted article is also included. For the rest, reviews, essays and position papers on issues of the day give the impression of a restless intelligence experimenting with various voices and stances, desperate for something to believe in. The Freudian, the Boy Scout, the Political Commissar,

the Fruity Englishman in Unlikely Places, the Rilkean sonneteer bashing out feminine rhymes while warplanes roar overhead – all give way, by the end of the decade, to the *émigré* detachment of America, and the chance to start again. But before that happens, certain markers have already been laid down as to the path he will afterwards follow.

If Eliot, a generation earlier, had projected himself back into an Italian thirteenth century to find his poetic terms of reference, for Auden it was the England of the eighteenth century. Instead of Iceland and China, or the glamour of Spain, the two key texts of the 'thirties are a superb essay on Pope and his times, and an equally powerful Introduction to the *Oxford Book of Light Verse*. These, like Eliot's pieces on Dante or the Elizabethans, are statements of poetic intent which far outweigh his political posturings of the day. The argument running through both is that Light Verse, of which the brilliant 'Letter to Lord Byron', Auden's finest contribution to *Letters from Iceland*, may be taken as an example, is the product of an integrated society freely, naturally and profitably expressing itself to itself. So called Serious Verse, of which the tortured lyricism of the Romantics is an example, is an outcome of social disintegration after the eighteenth century, the flight from the land, the centralisation of life in cities – in short, the arrival of the isolated modern individual, thrown back on his inner life and its private codified poetry, with no way through to an audience. The "inner life" then, like the compensatory need for "nature" poetry, are not natural in themselves but the outcome of social re-arrangement. 'Letter to Lord Byron' and these prose pieces, much more than the overtly political texts of the 'thirties, seem to me Auden's way of throwing down the gauntlet to a sick age, in the name of one that is not, or never was, alienated.

> A publisher's an author's greatest friend,
>   A generous uncle, or he ought to be.
> (I'm sure we hope it pays him in the end.)
>   I love my publishers and they love me,
>   At least they paid a very handsome fee
> To send me here. I've never heard a grouse
> Either from Russell Square or Random House.
>
>   ('Letter to Lord Byron')

Could anything be more breezily free of the sentiments most twentieth century poets entertain towards their publishers, or the age in general, than that? Yet it is entirely of a piece with Auden's need to imagine or believe himself into some ideal space such as, subsequently, the United States, "so large, so friendly and so rich" – where the poet, like any other labourer, is worthy of his hire. And alongside it go the willingness to de-mystify the act of writing in 'An Outline for Boys and Girls', to simplify things for children and tax authorities, to edit school magazines like *The Badger*, and to act as if what is, according to him, separated since the age of Pope, is once again connected:

> But whenever society breaks up into classes, sects, townspeople and peasants, rich and poor, literature suffers. There is writing for the gentle and writing for the simple, for the highbrow and the lowbrow; the latter gets cruder and coarser, the former more and more refined. And so, today, writing gets shut up in a circle of clever people writing about themselves for themselves, or ekes out an underworld existence, cheap and nasty. Talent does not die out, but it can't make itself understood. Since the underlying reason for writing is to bridge the gulf between one person and another, as the sense of loneliness increases, more and more books are written by more and more people, most of them with little or no talent.
> ('Outline for Boys and Girls')

As the 'thirties end and war and the 'forties approach, the single word "choice" recurs more and more frequently. There is a stronger and stronger sense of the distance between the Golden Age of instinct and innocence and the moral, conscious world where responsibility is the watchword. Aesthetics, in the Kierkegaardian sense, is giving way to ethics, and the shift of emphasis finds expression in two of the final texts he published before leaving for America in early 1939, the essay 'Morality in an Age of Change' and the sequence of poems 'In Time of War' with which this hugely readable volume closes:

> Wandering lost upon the mountains of our choice
> Again and again we sigh for an ancient South,
> For the warm nude ages of instinctive poise,
> For the taste of joy in the innocent mouth.
> ('In Time of War')

In Solitude, for Company, which takes up the story in America, is a much richer book than its unpromising subtitle of *Auden Studies 3* might suggest. There are uncollected texts on Freud, education and the Fall of Rome, a series of letters to his friend James Stern, a symposium on 'In Praise of Limestone', as well as descriptions and remembrances of his domestic life in the early 'forties, at 7 Middagh Street, Brooklyn, and later with Chester Kallman in Austria. While by no means adding up to a full biographical picture, it holds up a broken mirror to the later Auden, as *Prose 1926–1938* does to the younger man.

As always between two phases, there is change and there is continuity. Certain masks, for example that of the poet as politically engaged, are put aside with a kind of disgust, only to be replaced by others perhaps more fitting for the intellectually humbler though economically more rewarding American circuit, such as that of the Goethean sage able to discourse authoritatively on anything and everything. Only once is Auden brought up short, by an editor who suggests he is "living beyond his intellectual income" when refusing to publish a speech delivered at Swarthmore College on the theory of education. In general, though texts on teaching, psychoanalysis and classical civilisation might shock a specialist, they proceed intuitively, and are really pretexts for an airing of the poet's own contemporary concerns:

> Like the third century the twentieth is an age of stress and anxiety. In our case, it is not that our techniques are too primitive to cope with new problems, but the very fantastic success of our technology is creating a hideous, noisy, overcrowded world in which it is becoming increasingly difficult to lead a human life. In our reactions to this, one can see many parallels to the third century. Instead of gnostics, we have existentialists and God-is-dead theologians, instead of neo-Platonists, devotees of Zen, instead of desert hermits, heroin addicts and beats, instead of mortification of the flesh, sado-masochistic pornography...
> ('The Fall of Rome')

More important than the changes, though, are the continuities with the Auden of the 'thirties. One of them is his sense of himself as a professional poet, first outlined in the Pope essay of that previous decade, and in 'Letter to Lord Byron'. Working hours are an obsession, lecture tours, libretti and magazine articles a *modus vivendi*. In America as in

England earlier, there is an unchanging enthusiasm for collaboration. The MacNeices and Isherwoods of the 'thirties are replaced by the Kallmans and Stravinskys of the 'forties onwards. Collaboration in this narrow working sense is simply an element in Auden's fascination with marriage ("the *only* subject", as he wrote to James Stern) and his sense, after Kierkegaard, that the ethical will expressed in the marriage vow can dominate chance and fate. *Eros* can become *Agape*. As part of a larger search for order and integration it links too into the celebrations of domestic life in the 'sixties and 'seventies, not to mention the great earlier hymn to moderation that is 'In Praise of Limestone'. The ideal landscape of that poem, like the ideal eighteenth century of the Pope essay, has to yield, though, to the actual ugliness and chaos of late twentieth-century life. The pool in the limestone is, as Edna Longley points out, a private pool, and there is an increasing sense in the later Auden that only in the domestic, the interpersonal, is salvation to be found. The attempt to merge private and public, to believe in the poet as integral to some social fabric out of the eighteenth century, seems in the end to be unrealizable.

Neither of these books, for all the incidental light they throw on Auden's career, will provide definitive grounds for a judgement of his stature. Stan Smith's critical study, in a sense a paraphrase of the whole *oeuvre*, is a humbler attempt to come at the work and the man from the angle of the unschooled reader and should be judged differently. It suffers, in my view, from an excess of self-effacing modesty and a poor subdivision of the material, with biography, prose and poetry thrown together in slabs of undifferentiated prose broken up, incongruously, by section headings like 'Fumbled Embraces' and 'Buggering Off'. Conscientious stuff, but monochrome to a degree. Any rereading of a lifework like Auden's though, is liable to throw up a new notion or two, and Smith's emphasis on the "small group", be it the Downs School in the 'thirties or the Middagh Street *menage* of the 'forties – the lost community superseded by inhuman social environments – gets to the core of Auden's obsession with the eighteenth century, and his later despair at failure to find its living legacy in our own.

All of which brings us –provisionally, at least – back to Day Lewis's designation of his friend as the poetic giant of the century. But which century? If Auden could have switched places with the tortured visionary Christopher Smart, so beloved of the Beats and so out of his own time, literary history might have been a lot tidier. Possibly the twenty-first century, if it surprises us by being something other than the theatre of demonic forces this one has been, will name him as the Great Precursor of that society "integrated, but free" he so wished for, but which has yet to usher itself in.

Defying Gravity

by Lawrence Sail

HANS MAGNUS ENZENSBERGER

Kiosk

Translated by Michael Hamburger
Bloodaxe, £7.95
ISBN 1 85224 385 6

What's my purpose here? and what shall I say?
in what language? to whom?

THESE QUESTIONS, FROM the title poem of the earliest collection included in Enzensberger's *Selected Poems* (Bloodaxe, 1994) are still looking for answers in his highly enjoyable latest collection, which displays characteristic dynamism and wit. Something of the range is evident in the titles of the book's four sections: 'Historical Patchwork', 'Mixed Feelings', 'Diversions under the Cranium' and 'In Suspense'. Each section has a poem entitled 'Flight of Ideas' (numbered I to IV), a continuing meditation on the churning restlessness of creation. In a world in which nothing remains as it is, or repeats itself, "intentions hardly count", as three of the poems repeat, and there seems to be no escape, even though "You move house, flee, / mix with that / which is the case". The echo of Wittgenstein here (and in the fourth 'Flight of Ideas' poem) is apposite, as is the reminder of the double meaning of "flight": but it is the sense of taking wing which predominates in *Kiosk*. In 'Bird's Eye View', the view gained by height is of those who "contend with / the force of gravity" – yet the achievement of it is also "a mug's game", as futile perhaps as the bee in 'Humblebee, Bumble-bee' struggling to fly to freedom, but instead banging repeatedly against the windowpane – another climber come to grief, "A life for art's sake". 'An Observation on Shifts in Functional Elites' has the attempt to rise fatally undermined by fear, while the upward striving of 'New Man' who "clambers up words" results in nothing more than affinity with those he thinks he has superseded.

If all this climbing is, in one way or another, an attempt to fight clear of a world full of contradictions in which "restlessly the reactor of evolution looks / for new solutions, new hostages" ('Clinical Meditation'), the poems themselves are not escapist, but conspicuously witty, self-deprecatory, full of humanity and generosity. In the title poem, the three old ladies in the kiosk have the status of the Fates; 'For Karajan and Others' prizes three buskers in front of Kiev Station above the world of the concert hall. The laws of science, history, bureaucracy, the Fates, even perhaps God, all coexist with the facts of human uniqueness and persistence. Though the conscious mind may end up going in circles, as in 'Self-Demolishing Speech Act' ("With consummate ease / I refute all my refutations"), it can still be outflanked: as by the seven-year-old trampolinist in 'Presumption of Innocence' who, with others, "gets the better of gravity", and has thus momentarily managed to be "happy to the point of unconsciousness". And though haunted by past and future, the human animal can still call a halt amid the flux. "Don't move. Look", the poet instructs himself as he observes the light on a silver birch: and in 'The Somnambulist Ear', a wonderfully acute poem about noises heard by someone unable to sleep,

> you hear a whirring
> almost beyond the audible,
> phantasmally thin as the glittering ring
> of an unstoppable meter
>
> that revolves in the dark.

There are affinities in some of the poems with the energetic ferment of Peter Redgrove's work, and in others with the questing plainness of R.S. Thomas (with whom Enzensberger shares a liking for poems about paintings), but the variety and breadth of Enzensberger's thinking are entirely his own. They are well represented by his formal expertise: there are litanies reminiscent of Brecht, airy couplets, several poems consisting of a single sentence extending to up to 21 lines, even a rhymed sonnet. Throughout, Enzensberger maintains a lightness of tone which does not preclude intimacy, compassion or the elegiac reminiscence of such poems as 'Early Writings' and 'His Father's Ghost'. He is also well served by Michael Hamburger as his translator (though eight of the 70 poems here are translated by their author). It is a pity, all the same, that unlike the *Selected Poems*, this is not a bilingual edition. This would have enhanced some readers' enjoyment by enabling them to see how Enzensberger sometimes alters and adds to the German; and how Hamburger, while generally sticking close to the texts, shows touches of great inventiveness, as in offering equivalents rather than translations for Enzensberger's use of quotations from well known German poems. Thus Mörike ("Denk es, O Seele") becomes Clough ("Say not the struggle naught availeth"), while in 'Old Medium' quotations from poems by Goethe, Benn and Andreas Gryphius are cunningly matched with Shakespeare, Eliot and Bunyan respectively.

The book's final section comes close to a sense of the numinous: and the concluding poem, 'The Entombment', with its image of the rising butterfly, may remind us not only of the butterfly in Goethe's 'Selige Sehnsucht', and that poem's injunction "Stirb und werde!" ("Die and become!"), but of the idea of resurrection as another form of gravity-defying flight.

A Minor Splash

by Dennis O'Driscoll

Singers Behind Glass:
Eight Modern Dutch Poets

Selected and Translated by James Brockway,
Jackson's Arm, £7.99
ISBN 0 948282 16 9

A GOOD DEAL of contemporary poetry looks as if it has been bred in captivity rather than in the wild. Bloodless and bored, stunted and tame, it makes what Miroslav Holub describes as "diary-sized leaps of the imagination". Dangerous though it is to generalise about poetry which one is unable to read in the original, my impression is that modern Dutch verse is predominantly of the captive-bred variety. The poems are short – but without Brechtian bite – and they pace aimlessly around their pages as if vague about their purpose in life.

Awareness of Dutch-language poetry is not helped by the absence of a comprehensive survey anthology from a British publisher, so that readers will probably be more familiar with Romanian and Polish poets than with their neighbours across the North Sea. A scattering of individual volumes published in Britain (Faverey, Kopland, Claus, Roggeman, ten Berge) and Ireland (Achterberg, van Vliet) contained some interesting work from Dutch and Flemish poets; and the contributions of Judith Herzberg and Hans Verhagen, among others, are still memorable from the Dutch special issue of *Modern Poetry in Translation* two decades ago. Despite these welcome – if, on the whole, modest – discoveries, it is difficult to shake off the notion that, compared with the nation's painters, Dutch poets have made only a minor splash.

James Brockway's attractively-produced and useful compilation, *Singers Behind Glass*, does not purport to be a representative anthology but rather "a personal selection" of eight poets, ranging from the lyrical, melancholy, almost Hardyesque, J.C. Bloem (1887–1966) to an "off-hand, off-the-cuff" poet of absences, negatives and philosophical asides, Tom van Deel (born 1945). If Rutger Kopland is known to English readers, this will have much to do with Brockway's earlier exertions on his behalf, culminating in a full-length selection, *A World*

Beyond Myself (1991). At his best, Kopland (born 1934) can sustain a poignant, evocative note:

Silence, warm and summery, scent of hay,
of ditches, sound of cattle tearing
at the grass, of passionately singing birds,
an afternoon as for ever as a page.

Two of Kopland's poems are drawn from artists – not of the Dutch school, ironically, but from works by Leonardo and Michelangelo, poems which (like the ambiguous last line above) acknowledge the limitations of even the greatest art. Remco Campert's 'In Praise of Painters' records that "From my friends the painters / I learned how to look". Campert (born 1929) is associated with the 'fifties generation, which loosened the necktie of traditional Dutch poetry in favour of a less formal, more spontaneous style (surrealism and dadaism were among the favoured stimulants of the movement, though used sparingly by Campert himself).

The skewed intensities of Gerrit Achterberg's poetry present the translator with tremendous challenges. Explaining his own reluctance to translate him in bulk, Brockway comments that "Form and content in his case are so finely fused together that I did not want to interfere by putting his words into a language other than his own". Treating language as a kind of elaborate combination lock, Achterberg (1905–62) desperately seeks the conjunction of words which will release from death the woman he murdered. His poems exude a powerful sense of time as the element which separates him from his beloved, who is now out of time: "Dark, your objects gleam in me, / heavy with eternity: / death can differ no whit from this / except that here I still possess / time, in which it settles down, / becomes a poem".

Less impressive and less obsessive than Achterberg's work is the romantic poetry of the eternally young Hans Lodeizen (1924–1950). The best of the selection is the hedonistic portrait, 'Evening at the Merrills" (Lodeizen was personally acquainted with James Merrill), in which the needle hovers between send-up and celebration. At 32 lines, the poem is virtually an epic by the standard of these distinctly short-winded poets – as is the 28-line 'The Idiot in the Bath' by M. Vasalis (born 1909). A pseudonymous psychiatrist, like Rutger Kopland, Vasalis is not without sympathy for her "idiot" but is not without scientific detachment either; she does not allow "The clouds of vapour rising from the trough" to mist the eyes or soften the focus.

With Anton Korteweg (born 1944), the pain frequently consists of what Thom Gunn calls "the ultimate pain / of feeling no pain". Korteweg's poem, 'Punishment' reads in full: "Every single thing goes right for me. / Wife, pen, bike – it all just sails along. / I get promoted simply sitting down. / What is it then I did so very wrong?"

Usually sceptical, sometimes cynical, often witty, Korteweg brings the daily world of CDs and PCs, Garfield and Lego, work and marriage – not much in evidence elsewhere in the book – to his poems like a breath of fresh air. By the end of 'Cycling to Work', a reverie on love as he pedals from Leiden to The Hague, he is actually out of breath; along with another poem on the theme of love, the convincingly diffident 'Request Number', its qualities make one regret that a poet of such obvious gifts does not stretch his talents to produce work that demands more – in the way of form, imagery, vision, scope – than Brockway's selection from his output suggests. If Korteweg is a representative figure among contemporary Dutch poets, then lack of conviction may be a greater problem than lack of talent. The cage is of their own making.

Jackson's Arm, Sunk Island Publishing, PO Box 74, Lincoln LN1 1QG

TWO POEMS BY ANTON KORTEWEG

TUNNELS

Use the tunnel, it says. You do, and read:
Astrid, I love you. Fine. So far, so good.
Diving under the main road into the wood:
Astrid, you rotten whore! Negative erection.

This way, at half-past eight in the morning,
within ten minutes you can move from the most banal
expression of love to the coarsest gob of disgust.
In real life it takes from five to seven years.

FATHER

When he's grown big, I'll get a car.
Saturday mornings he can wash it down for me.
And a lawn. That's for him to mow.

I'll drive old ladies into the street.
Then he can help them cross the road.
Young lads onto dangerous ice,
for him to rescue at the risk of his life.

One day anyhow I'll have to learn what it is
to tap him approvingly on the shoulder,
look him in the eye and, blushing, murmur:
My boy, your father's proud of you.

Translated from the Dutch by James Brockway.

NEW POETS '97

GEE WILLIAMS

I WAS BORN in North Wales to parents for whom literature was big – not with a capital "l", though, but with a small "b" for books: H. G. Wells, Edgar Wallace got equal treatment in our house – they were on the same shelf, right? My father died at "A" Level time – I thought that was it, but Culham College (so far out of Oxford it might have been attached to Reading) took a chance on me and after three years and a final one at Exeter College I got my degree. That last year my tutor was a young man called Michael O'Neill. He was researching Shelley and infected me with an interest that has remained ever since. There was another factor that made my undergraduate years slightly different: a month before I was due to leave home I married my boyfriend who was already up at Jesus College. We're still together but I've missed all that Wendy Cope stuff on having a broken heart. I've always written short fiction and poetry and the former's been broadcast or published for fifteen or more years. (I got a 1995 Rhys Davies Contemporary Short Story Prize). But the poetry I've only started to let out during the 'nineties.

ON BEING GIVEN A ROMAN FIBULA

(lost in York circa 80 A.D.)

He will have used some foul obscenity
current and in vogue with the common men
serving amongst the savagery and cold
– oh northern cold – from which his high nomen
had failed to garner him and keep sun-shored:

words for a captured Pictish tart's red bits
or the well-used bum of his boss's Gallic boy,
oaths that were screamed when steam and comfort failed
or another tribe arrived to thieve, destroy
or defecate upon the clean stones laid.

Or had he knowledge of a minor god?
A little cult the legionaries blessed
with wine and blood, a deity of lost
and wanted things to whom he now confessed
his carelessness and lobbied. Who stayed deaf.

SHELLEY DROWNING

This trick of water in its thick, sly push
has haunted my waking time . . . has slapped my
face for staring and snapped and sealed the lids.
It has smothered a too-familiar voice.
If I look into its eye it offers
dreams: conjuring with my weight, levitates
and lets slip as my fear soaks up a stuff
clearer and lighter than the infant soul.

The waves have found out my affair with earth.
This guile of clarity Democritus saw:
his atoms ever looser in their loves
through seeping space, a hollow far from shore.

LOVE AND PRINZ OPTICS

Out on the dark lawn you have for me
the rings of Saturn that open and close,
trapped in a squat lens even as they return
and twist and turn to their cold apogee.

Not the best time. Tense, through still space you stalk
near-perfect an aspect presented to
the Earth, brilliant and sharp, for this fat-god's
licentious festival . . . his embellished
globe presenting to me its icy torques

each glittering about immensity,
pin-point and slant. Out on the dark lawn
you slip around my wrists the braided rings
of Saturn that hold fast a far known world:
located, gazeteered, switched on for me.

Crashing the Devil's Party

by Michael Donaghy

Rebel Angels:
25 Poets of the New Formalism
Edited by Mark Jarman and David Mason
Story Line Press, $12
ISBN 1 885266 30 8

LOOKING FOR CONVOLUTED tribal hierarchies, kinship rituals, and creation myths? Why parachute into some unhygienic rain forest when the culture of American poetry is an anthropologist's Disneyland? Here, segregated into traditions of the Raw, under the totem of Whitman, and the Cooked, under Dickinson, almost every poet declares an allegiance to his or her tribe or "movement". In Britain a group of poets could once afford to call themselves simply *the* Movement. But in America poets survive, courtesy of the university syllabus, insofar as they can be grouped under headings like "The New York School", "Beats" "Confessionals", "Objectivists" ("You must have a movement", Harriet Monroe warned a reluctant Louis Zukovsky, "Give it a name".) A loner hasn't much chance in this game. The best way to pass your poetic genes on to the next generation is to get yourself classified, ranked, and anthologised.

This looks a serviceable anthology for next year's seminar: *Rebel Angels* – a crimson book jacket adorned with a suitably intense image from Blake –*The Good and Evil Angels Struggling for Possession of a Child*. You'd be forgiven for thinking it some wild raw word salad tossed up by Iain Sinclair. Except that it's full of sonnets. These are what editors Jarman and Mason consider the best of New Formalism, a movement christened, like many literary and artistic movements of the past, by its opponents. If that's not confusing enough, consider the title of the book in relation to the cover illustration. Surely the rebel angels are Satan's Legions, and in Blake's picture it's the evil angel who is losing possession of the child (the public? the Academy? the point?) Just who do these angels think they are?

For all their striking differences, both New Formalism and Language poetry emerged in 'eight-

ies America as formalist reactions to the typical magazine or writing program verse of the period – a brief free verse confessional lyric of the sort promoted by the Writing Programs. In their Preface, Jarman and Mason sketch out the background. They recount the explosion of spleen when New Formalism was first acknowledged as a movement around 1985 and the teaching poets rallied round to condemn the upstarts. If one agrees with Valéry that one of the chief pleasures of rhyme is the rage it inspires in its opponents, these attacks make for a diverting read. But how to account for the peculiar intensity of this rage?

It's hard to imagine America's literary inferiority complex before the advent of Modernism, now that the roles are reversed and America the dominant world culture. But it fuelled Whitman's campaign to free American literary language from "the burden of the past" (England, in this context), a task resumed by an obsessively Anglophobic William Carlos Williams. In the 'sixties Williams was regarded as the patron saint of the Raw school, whose adherents took on board his literary nationalism and its complex of myths – that Whitman is the poet favoured by the common man, for example, or that free verse is a kind of magic spell which liberates the oppressed (something of this latter notion survives in Language poetry – the belief that writing a poem entirely composed from punctuation marks will help bring down the arms trade). Jarman and Mason quote a 1986 attack on the New Formalists by Diane Wakowski in which she warns of a plot to undermine "the free verse revolution and the poetry which is the fulfilment of the Whitman heritage" (Dr Williams' rage against Eliot's "betrayal", one recalls, was couched in similar terms). And she denounces John Hollander as "Satan". Is this the meaning of Jarman and Mason's crimson cover? Perhaps the New Formalists need to present themselves as Satanic, as worthy of a *fatwah*, in order to register as a chapter in literary history.

But when is formalism progressive and when is it reactionary? Few of the poets in this anthology would admit to using form to invoke a spurious historical authority. And many poets considered *avant garde* have experimented with the restrictions of form. Is there any real difference between Language poet Ron Silliman's strict adherence to a mathematical sequence and Thom Disch's use of the alphabet as a formal device? Perhaps it's all a matter of intention: poem as *utterance* vs. poem as seminar topic. Jarman and Mason probably wouldn't designate Ashbery a New Formalist though he's employed such highly conventional forms as the pantoum and sestina as "devices for getting into remoter areas of consciousness". "The really bizarre requirements of a sestina", he told *New York Quarterly*, "I use as a probing tool rather than as a form in the traditional sense...rather like riding downhill on a bicycle and having the pedals push your feet. I wanted my feet pushed into places they wouldn't normally have taken". But surely this is *precisely* the function of "form in the traditional sense" – that serendipity provided by negotiation with a resistant medium, the intervention of what we used to call the muse. Compare Ashbery's strict adherence to the poetry handbook with the methods of those Old Formalists of the 'fifties (then called the New Formalists). I said this got convoluted) who rarely succumbed to this kind of foot fetish. "Though I commonly work in meters", wrote Richard Wilbur, "my way of going about a poem is very like the free verse writer's: that is, I begin by letting the words find what line lengths seem right to them... All of my poems, therefore, are formally *ad hoc*; quite a few are, so far as I know, without formal precedent, and none sets out to fulfil the rules of some standard form". Perhaps the old new formalists were of the Devil's party without knowing it, as Blake said of Milton. To confuse matters further, *Rebel Angels* contains many poems in experimental or "procedural" forms: we find Dana Gioia adapting a fugue form used by Weldon Kees, for example, Thom Disch exhausting the permutations of a rhyme scheme, and Marilyn Hacker forging a minimalist verse form out of a line from *The Snow Queen*.

Apart from these poets already familiar to British readers, *Rebel Angels* offers all too brief a glimpse of Marilyn Nelson, Charles Martin, R.S. Gwynn, Greg Williamson, and Rachel Wetzsteon. I was delighted to discover Molly Peacock, whose giddily enjambed rhymes drive her erotic poems like a dynamo – commendably erotic in that Ms Peacock doesn't want to display or exploit desire, she wants to *understand* it, and rhyme is her vehicle. Mary Jo Salter displays a similar command of technique. In 'Welcome to Hiroshima' she writes of wandering that city's Peace Park, dismayed by the kitsch, until she stops before a display of a sliver of glass:

...a shard the bomb slammed
in a woman's arm at eight-fifteen, but some
three decades on – as if to make it plain

hope's only renewable as pain,
and as if all the unsung
debasements of the past may one day come
rising to the surface once again –
worked its filthy way out like a tongue.

Rhyme imitates the symmetry of logic, and here Salter exploits this to reinforce her rhetoric in a technique analogous to a musical cadence. She interrupts the sentence and the concrete image it conveys to shift to an abstract register – future and past, hope and guilt – like a suspension bridge across the stanza break before resolving on a single obscenely visceral simile.

Despite their explanations, the editor's selection policy eludes me. Where, for example, is Gjertrud Schnackenberg? Brooks Haxton? Vikram Seth? Tim Steele is here, but not his excellent 'Sapphics Against Anger'; the blank verse narratives of Andrew Hudgins and Sydney Lea take up so many pages one wishes for a separate anthology of "New Narrative" poetry; and – this is disturbingly familiar – poets born before 1940 are excluded by fiat. What's more, there's enough forced rhyme and inert metrically woozy rhythm in this anthology to suggest that the American ear has atrophied. Elizabeth Alexander reads like Marilyn Hacker rhyming in her sleep; Bruce Bawer takes most of a sonnet to look out of a plane window and compare the lights below to stars – something that must have occurred to anyone who's ever flown; one could easily imagine Phyllis Levin swapping personifications with Abraham Cowley: "On the border of the future / Broods the infinite / There knowledge slowly sips her wine / And savors it". I hasten to add that Levin redeems herself with 'The Lost Bee' but hers is a grey lonesome world: "It was my love upon the bed / who pointed out my silhouette / Anonymous and monochrome". All too often in *Rebel Angels* that tone of world-weary sophistication intrudes like a sepia pall, as though the climb up Parnassus were too exhausting and the view from the summit a disappointment. Compare this to the new poets writing over here whose use of form signals an increase of energy and momentum.

Rebel Angels contains many surprises and is worth having on your bookshelf. If the ground has shifted during this past decade and American poetry has become more formal across the board, the movement was a success and their anthology can lay it to rest. Rebels or not, the best of these poets deserve better than to be bundled in a pigeonhole.

Flavors of Mortality

by Helen Dunmore

THOMAS LYNCH

The Undertaking: Life Studies from the Dismal Trade

Cape, £9.99
ISBN 0 224 04276 9

AS A CHILD, Thomas Lynch believed that it was his father's profession to take the dead underground. To take someone somewhere is to accompany them, even to give support to them on their journey. Although Lynch soon realised his childish mistake, and that his father did not go down among the dirt and bones each time a funeral took place, he later came to see in the error a deeper truth about the work his father did. Lynch has inherited the profession, and with it he has chosen the profession of poetry. Another part of his inheritance is the house in West Clare from which his great-grandfather emigrated to America a hundred years ago. Lynch has a powerful sense of what it is to break from tradition, and to return to it. For all his family's long history in America, its Irish Catholic roots feed a sharp, everyday consciousness of life shaped by coming death. Lynch writes about the likely fates of body and soul with force, humour, and an easy lack of embarrassment.

An undertaker without tradition is an unimaginable creature. There must be black clothes, efficiency without bustle, an ability to choreograph the grieving family without appearing to do so, and a sound, experienced grasp of human behaviour in the face of death. There must also be an understanding of form. In a poem and in a funeral, form is used to organise the unwieldy mass of human emotion into a shape which is both apt and memorable. Lynch suggests that the undertaker's responsibility to the families of the dead goes beyond the social, into the aesthetic and indeed the spiritual. Through a thousand practical details, he accompanies those who are learning to be widows or orphans.

But if undertaking is a profession, it is also a business. There must be itemised bills, and Lynch acknowledges that they are large ones. He is sensitive to the lampooning American funeral directors have suffered from Jessica Mitford, Evelyn Waugh and other critics of mawkish procedure and excessive profit. Certainly, Lynch's own profit margin of five per cent seems modest. He writes from a small township, a place where the dead are almost always known to the living. In handling them, Lynch recognises them, telling over their stories to himself as he prepares them for burial. One of the most unflinching passages deals with the Lynch brothers' embalming and undertaking of their own father. As Lynch observes, "We act out things we cannot put into words".

Lynch judges his tone very carefully. He sounds intimate, but he is not confessional, even when he alludes to alcoholism, marriage break-up, and loneliness. The book rarely takes us down into the underworld of raw emotion. Lynch prefers anecdote, description and opinion, and is at his best when looking outward, as he does in his dry but comradely disquisition on the hypochondria of his fellow poet, Matthew Sweeney. This is a wonderfully comic chapter. Lynch muses on Sweeney's "rare antennae for the flavors of mortality, a keen aptitude for the taste of survival", while the poets share sashimi and debate death from fugu poisoning. Lynch's satisfactoriness as a companion on these jaunts is clear; when faced with detailed questioning on the various forms of death, he observes that: "I have long thought it my professional duty, when questioned by someone of Matthew's sensibilities, either to give the true answer when it is known to me, or to suggest a source in the topical literature where such an answer might be found, or, failing either of these, to make something up".

Lynch comes across as a deeply humane man, educated in the humanities by both his professions. If at times he sounds a little too avuncular, a little too proprietorial about the death which in the end belongs to everyone, it becomes clear that he sees himself fighting against a culture which is losing its sense of how to die, and how to bury the dead. He may seem to repeat himself in his insistence throughout the book that death is not part of the "choice" culture to which we cling, but this insistence has to be set in the context of cryogenics, euthanasia and the desperate plastic surgery which tries to buy off old age. His argument that the unwillingness to look at death leaves us death-haunted is a powerful one, and the more so for being so richly and readably expressed.

Myth Kitty Revisited

by Maggie O'Farrell

JAMES HARPUR

The Monk's Dream

Anvil, £7.95

ISBN 0 85646 278 0

IN MY MORE cynical moments I get impatient with poets who rely heavily on imagery and stories drawn from mythology. I cannot suppress the suspicion that overuse of classical metaphors represents a poetical cop-out: mythology provides a stock of themes that can be plundered at any moment. Like people who hire designer furniture for parties, some poets indulge in a bit of rent-an-image to give themselves an academic air, as if including a couched reference to Ovid somehow validates their writing. When faced with such a poem, I feel like a code-breaker: once you've identified the myth – congratulations! – you've got the poem, you can collect your two hundred pounds.

I felt, then, a slight foreboding when faced with James Harpur's new collection. But Harpur's use of classical allusion is gentle, sentient, profound and above all secondary to his main concern. Harpur is grappling with a conundrum more challenging than code-breaking – his whole collection represents a struggle with the question of mortality.

In 'The Flight of the Sparrow', he sends Bede's sparrow once more through the draughty hall (surely one of the most overworked allusions in poetry?): a courtier describes life and "the mysteries of the afterlife" as a brief, fleeting "dart" of a sparrow through a hall in winter. Briefly "cocooned in light and warmth," the sparrow "can enjoy a moment's calm / Before it vanishes, rejoining / The freezing night from which it came". It ends with a misleading tone of resignation: "Beyond the doors of birth and death / We are completely in the dark". Misleading because Harpur cannot leave it at that: death fascinates him. Like Hamlet, he circles again and again around the anxiety of what happens after death. In an echo of Browning's Bishop, his "paestum diver" orders that "sensuality stain / This cool ascetic tomb". But although he wants "scenes of my

funeral feast...my old companions...release their tongues with wine", he professes nothing but disdain for the secular, physical world to which they belong. In the face of death, he envisages himself as pure, stripped of sin, "diving through my sensate life / To the waters of oblivion". The idea of a Christian cleansing of the soul attends many of Harpur's poems, but it seems to spring less from a judgmental religiousness than a philanthropic concern for the souls of his fellow beings. The royal advisor in 'The Monk's Dream' is left to ponder predestination and the foolishness of "testing God" after King William refuses to heed an omen and is struck down by an arrow. The nameless speaker urges: "we must cleanse our lives of blood. / Do penance for transgressions of the past..."

At the centre of the book is the sonnet sequence about his father's death, 'Frame of Furnace Light'. It is an extraordinary piece of writing, beginning with a series of lantern slide glimpses of the father, remembered solely because his illness has had the curious effect of returning to him his identity. Harpur represents his father with such clarity and sympathy as to render his gradual decline almost unbearable. The most affecting sonnets are the ones which concentrate on the father–son relationship and all that is unspoken between them: watching a rugby match, "magiked inside a sunlit television / we sit apart...And in the silence we are locked as one / Gripped by the infectious currents of the play". The son is a master of restraint; it is only in a poem, 'Gilgamesh and the Death of Enkidu' that we witness the unbound grief to which he might have liked to have given full rein: "'You cannot die. I will not let you go'... For several days Gilgamesh wept and shivered...felt his power drain away".

Lazarus is an irresistible subject for Harpur. There is more than a glimmer of hope in Lazarus' account of the enlightenment attained after death: "A gradual joy blossomed / Grew irrepressible...Like wine glugging uncontrollably / From the throat of a jar knocked over. / Then the world appeared in sudden clarity". In place of the image of a sparrow's onward flight into oblivion, we are presented with a man dragged back to the shackles of physical existence. The poem contains an interesting idea, as an apparent aside: that the telling and retelling of a story can destroy the reality of the event. Lazarus laments that "each time my story comes to life...I am resurrected / into death by repetition". There's a lesson in that for anyone who thinks they might be coming over all mythological.

Rhulterig

by Ian McMillan

MATTHEW FRANCIS

Blizzard

Faber, £6.99
ISBN 0 571 17854 5

TRACEY HERD

No Hiding Place

Bloodaxe, £6.95
ISBN 1 85224 381 3

TOBIAS HILL

Midnight in The City of Clocks

Oxford Poets, £6.99
ISBN 0 19283 245 X

JAMES KEERY

That Stranger, The Blues

Carcanet, £8.95
ISBN 1 85754 321 2

KATRINA PORTEOUS

The Lost Music

Bloodaxe, £6.95
ISBN 1 85224 380 5

AH, THE REVIEWER's dilemma, hunched over the freshly unJiffybagged new books, poring over them like a child at Christmas with a floor-full of new toys: how do you find the words? Here are the slim volumes, the new poets fresh from the mould and there's no point, no point at all, in dragging out the tired old phrases because these aren't tired old poets. So: no Promising, no Individual Voice, no Oddly Mature. No Crafted, no Aware of Tradition, no Iconoclast. So what, then, clever clogs. We'll have to see. Maybe Rhulterig will do. Maybe.

Matthew Francis

Matthew Francis is studying the poetry of W. S. Graham and maybe it shows a little bit, maybe his poems are a wee bit Grahamy, but it doesn't really matter, because they're more Francish than Grahamy, which adds up to a fine dose of Rhulterig.

If you're confused about Rhulterig that's because I've just invented it. It means, loosely, The Quality Which Makes Poems Completely Belong to The Poet Who Wrote Them. It means that the poems fit the poet like a glove fits a hand or a barge fits a canal. So a poem like 'Winter Road' begins in a Francish way, with precise observation and off-kilter vision combining in a rich Rhulterig soup: "Driving along the road / I see the black wires / that held the leaves together, / how Summer's trick was done. / / England always reverts to Winter". That last sentence is perfect within the context of the poem, which is maybe all we can ask of a sentence in a poem, and Francis's poems are full of such perfection, a kind of self-confidence, a steam of knowingness round the poem's boiling kettle: "A convention of moths applauded / the lamp they had come so far to see" ('Towards midnight'); "Early risers get to know / the wind that makes their shadows blow" ('Small hours'); "That's the best thing about coming here: the scenery doesn't wait to be looked at" ('A blind man in a forest'). It seems that Francis is seeking to make poems out of, if not exactly discarded things, then un-noticed things. Many of the poems work well, and the Rhulterig isn't too tight a fit.

Tracey Herd

If Francis's poems are Francish with a sprinkle of Grahamy, then Tracey Herd's writing is definitely Bloodaxed, and I mean that in the nicest possible way. Bloodaxe poets have a certain Rhulterig that's easy to spot; a wisdom, a knowingness, an at-ease-with language strut. Herd is a Scottish poet but her subjects are international. Here's Marilyn Monroe getting out of a swimming pool: "He made her do the same scene / fifty times. Flashbulbs / light up her face / as she slips in and out / of the water with barely / a wrinkle of blue". The writing is precise, tight, wearing its redrafting as lightly as possible, although I suspect that many of the lines have been in and out of the water as often as Marilyn. Herd's Herdiness is her ability to create stories, monologues, that lift the lid on odd worlds you'd like to know more about: "She appeared to me twice in one evening / like the moon spreading across a snow-field / blue and freezing, electric at its edges" ('The Snow Storm'). "An ocean cracks against the rocks. / The thoroughbred's nostril's flare / wide and red: her taut flanks / spray as the sweat breaks / in an arc..." ('The Nightmare of the Gallops Watcher'). Part of Herd's Rhulterig is a kind of Raymond Chandler persona, a fascination with detective stories, but I have to say that I found the non-hard boiled work in the book much more exciting. Maybe I've been coshed on the head too many times.

Tobias Hill

Tobias Hill is Tobiased, and his travel poems are Hilly. As the blurb says, he's "young and much travelled", and although those two things needn't make you into a good poet, in Hill's case they have. In his fascination with making phrases there's a Francish steam (see earlier) around many of Hill's poems and a boyish glow in their eagerness to be new: "Today the world is ugly: through Holloway and Kentish town / the bike bag-lady is riding / with a fishtank on her knees. / In the fishtank is a bone. / She stops outside the library. / She talks the snarl of wind in kitestring". I like that entire stanza but I especially like that last line: it seems to be complete Rhulterig in that lesser writers wouldn't have attempted it, wouldn't have knitted the line from the woman to the kite to the sound of her voice. Like Francis and Herd, Hill is confident, and maybe that's a consequence of the new perceived popularity of poetry: our young poets are confident of an audience, confident of a hearing by sets of informed ears. Actually, Hill is so confident that when he writes about a fat, sweaty Sumo Wrestler, the writing actually appears to be fat and sweaty, and that's full Rhulterig: "One salmon-egg, a boil or pearl, / sticks to his doll-lips. He presses its flat with his elephant fingertips. // Licks it. The barclock is too thin / between minutes, / and the floor mat / learns flatness under his weight. / His thighs flop down like sunstruck apes".

Hill wins a lot of competitions, and his poems have that winning ability to stand on their own, as if on stilts and in brightly-coloured jackets. If 'July 14th, 10pm' hasn't won a competition, then it deserves to, or at least the first stanza does: "The moon round as an oven-dial. / Ten fire-engines slide their red trombones / up past the Cock and Bottle / and the brink-lights of petrol-stations".

James Keery

I've got to admit that I'm a fan of James Keery's, and his Keery poems have livened up many a dull magazine. If Rhulterig really does mean that the poems fit the poet like a glove then in James Keery's case it means that they fit him like skin. He's unlike most other poets in his serious playfulness, his chronicling of a flaky part of Lancashire as though it's the centre of the universe, like Nicholson's

Millom or Mackay Brown's Orkneys, as in 'Aspull Common': "I noticed yesterday on Aspull Common / That it appeared to rise a bit more steeply / and take in more around than I recalled, but it's astonishing to see how much". Many of the poems are like that, in their innocence and ingenuousness, their wide-eyedness, their Keer: "It was clear dusk to one who had been outside, / Doubtless dark already to those who were / about to draw the curtains in brilliant rooms". The poems draw you in, make you forget your critical faculties, feel as open as the first lick of an ice cream. As well as landscape and birdwatching, Keery writes marvellously about teaching: "Not least of the small, incidental pleasures / Of having the school library to look after / has been to learn that there is in existence / A library classification system called Bliss, // and a variation of it called Modified Bliss. / I have found teaching English, on the whole, / despite all its frustrations, to be bliss- / and even at its worst, well-modified bliss!" I guess that Keery's work will never be fashionable but I also guess that's the way he likes it. He won't like the idea of Rhulterig because he didn't think of it himself, and that's why I like his work.

Katrina Porteous

The Lost Music has been justly praised all over the place for its Porteousness, for its reclaiming of lost lives, for the way it celebrates a history that is falling into the sea. I agree that Katrina Porteous's work fits her completely in a Rhulteriggish way, and I rejoice that poems like 'Five Sea Songs' can take their place in the clattering Poetry Kitchen alongside the other poems mentioned in this review: "Wund's freshening', bonny lass- / Boats'll no be off the morn. / Ah'll bide abed aside on ee / an' hear ye breathe abeyn the storm". In many of the poems Porteous is chronicling the lives of the fishermen of the Northumberland village of Beadnell, and her poetic act of rescue becomes an emblem, maybe, for the way poetry can be important as we stagger towards the millennium: it can reclaim the lost things, from these fishermen to Keery sunsets over Leigh RLFC, to Hilly visions of Japan, Herdy memories of a Scottish childhood and Francish visions of bee-filled nights. Or, as Porteous puts it in the title poem of the collection: "There is a place where it is all recorded. / Each look, each touch and kiss, each word, discarded / as casually as rain into the sea, is treasured there, and waits to be recovered". And the place is Rhulterig.

Burns Stanza

by Sheenagh Pugh

IAIN CRICHTON SMITH

The Human Face

Carcanet, £7.95

ISBN 1 857542517

FOR ONCE, THE back-cover blurb is true. "An impassioned poem-essay in Burns' most celebrated poetic form" is an exact description, and what makes it "ambitious and risky" is both the fact that it *is* impassioned, and the difficulty of the form. We are talking "Standard Habbie" here, the form Burns popularised though he didn't invent it; the form of "To a Louse", "Holy Willie's Prayer" and umpteen others. In his hands it looks so flowing, so conversational, so damn *easy* that one is tempted to try. I have, for years, and got nowhere. It's only when you *do* try that the problems of finding four a-rhymes and two b-rhymes each verse, plus staying in a metre more restrictive than it looks, become apparent. To attempt to keep it up for over 300 verses is ambitious, all right.

I think it would be amazing if he did, and there are points where the form stumbles. It doesn't really matter that many of the rhymes are approximate – Burns's are, often enough. It does look unnatural when he starts hunting rhymes in French. I know Scots English does accommodate certain French-derived words, but when it comes to –

> just like yourself; your sad confrère
> who has his place on this drenched terre,
> who is to father, mother, chèr
> as you to yours

– it looks contrived. (The accent on "chèr" is in the text, by the way). There are metrical glitches too: I find it hard to read "deus ex machina sent / to untangle a dénouement" in this or any rhythm, and the device of splitting words, fun in itself, can become exhausting to read when taken this far:

> which is more important then,
> plumber or plasterer or en-
> gineer, watchmaker or Gen-
> uine tailor,

actor, actress, prince or senatorial

It is when the poem is at its most "impassioned" that the form works best, and you see why he chose it. It is Burns' spirit of democracy, pacifism and humanity which is evoked; this is a denunciation of all dogmas, political and religious, in whose name men kill each other. They could not do so, I think Crichton Smith believes, if they looked into each other's faces and saw their common humanity. I am not sure everyone is as kind as that, but one cannot but be moved by his conviction:

> ...That twisted face
> contorted by your ethics is
> your human brother, not a prize
> for your revolver.
> See how his scared uncertain eyes
> fearfully waver.

On the waste of human life and the "phantom heaven" which blinds men to the joys of life on earth, the poem is consistently that impassioned and eloquent. Things being as they are, he is actually taking more of a risk with this than with the form. As someone says in today's paper, nothing dates a product nowadays more than lack of irony. I met a lauded young poet, once, who said he wouldn't write the conviction poetry he wanted to because "it isn't fashionable; it isn't cool". I nearly spat. If you want cool, it isn't here. This is heated, engaged, heartfelt, and about something that matters. That's probably why it can survive some awkwardness (and some dodgy proof-reading). I wish the end were stronger. "And let our last affirmative view / be like Rome or Florence" doesn't lodge in my mind, perhaps because I've never seen either. The extra syllable in the last line is a pity, too. But there is enough that *does* lodge:

> And who would see them as he dies –
> those socketless, unjewelled eyes,
> that buzzing bustle of black flies
> and legless bodies,
> and with blind arrogance confess:
> "Those were my studies
>
> as scholar and experimenter,
> chemist, scientist, inventor.
> I cut them off from life's adventure
> for such a reason..."

Exquisite Displacement

by Andrew Zawacki

DAVID HARTNETT

At the Wood's Edge

Cape, £7.00
ISBN 0 224 04158 4

JAMIE McKENDRICK

The Marble Fly

Oxford Poets, £6.99
ISBN 0 19 283256 5

CHARTING THE WIDE spaces of memory and loss, the natural world, domestic tranquillity and its underside of ennui, Hartnett's fourth collection *At the Wood's Edge* nonetheless suffers by being too safe in its distance: the poems are subservient to diminishing formal constraints. In 'Hoard' he describes creativity in sartorial terms:

Her cloths of gold, her coat of many shades...
Spring's white cotton nightdress rucked to the hips,
Summer's transparent basque satinning a breast,
Brown silks of autumn a long thigh strains taut,
Winter's creaking leathers unzipped to the waist.

The trope of the weather as clothing is itself worn thin, nor is it stitched more beautifully here for its sensuality made sexual. The unmediated movement from spring to winter is predictable, and the end-stopped lines further the monotony by preventing any torque or turning between phrases. The passage might have been saved had its rhythm lulled us through the seasons, but the third and fourth lines are awkward and nervous in their dactylic gestures.

Elsewhere his metaphors overreach, making their sublime pretensions nearly ridiculous. In one poem "that diligent editor Time / Returns every submission", and in 'Interstice', where the world must wait to resume its motion until a woman in a sunhat has returned, wasps are

Sullenly obliged to float at anchor
Before they can embark once more upon

Their malignant piracies, raiding the coasts
Of dusty chestnut archipelagoes.

Hartnett occasionally alights on compelling descriptions, as when cable cars are "hung on their hawsers' braided necklaces", or when jellyfish in their "frilled skirts" form a "fleet of liquid cupolas". Often, however, the poems stumble in search of a darkness or illumination which eludes them, as in the Latinate diction of "an oak in sections lies", the arch profundity of asking about the birds, "What had the grey ones chattered?" or the Prufrockian query, "Did my jeans still have flares?"

The 15-part World War I elegy 'Wreaths' and the 'Day of the Dead Deer' sequence are more ambitious, yet even their crucial moments fall short: the spirit of the deer cries, *"Dismembered...disembered disremembered",* and the whole event is called a "complex orchestration" in the woods' "amphitheatre", down to the "primitive harp" of the ribcage and the "clarinet stops of two black hooves". Poems such as 'Breaking and Entering' might have evinced a casual terror, but they are offset by redundancy: the narrator wonders of the intruder, "Had he been made, quite suddenly, a ghost? / I shivered then. It was time to be afraid". Hartnett pursues the shadows cast by the quotidian and the light which shines briefly through the intimacy and vulnerability of love, but his saying-so is forced, and the volume disappoints despite its scope of felt and imagined experience.

Jamie McKendrick

The Marble Fly is a collection of exquisite displacement. Like the so-called "century plant", an agave in the Oxford Botanical Gardens, McKendrick "holds grimly on" to his "patch of nowhere"

as though there were no belonging anywhere
but there and then, and nothing sublime
except that stretch of dirt, that broken wall
and the rays of a faded nineteenth-century sun.

His third volume runs the gamut from Roman antiquity and Old Testament plagues to D-Day. A diaspora of personalities, from Abel and Euclid to the Emperor Maximilian and even John Ashbery, waiting for a taxi, floats through its disquietude unhindered and unobtrusively, as though time were merely an anaesthetised slipstream. Yet this is not a poetry of populace: a singular consciousness hidden in the arras pulls the strings, revealing itself occasionally by an anxious laugh or a nervous twitch.

The "shards and rags and scraps" of this defamiliarized world are all too familiar: empty hotel rooms, stale toast and tobacco threads impart both despair and a disconcerting contentment. In 'Name-Tag' McKendrick describes an institution somewhere between a mental asylum and an army barracks, or a hospital and a boys' public school, where, "Mornings, we get a tick for shitting / after the prefect has inspected it". The vague titles 'Person Unknown,' 'Somewhere Please' and 'Six Characters in Search of Something' wrongfoot us from the start. Haunted by hearses, the first plane, a rubber dinghy and a stolen bike, the book is tense with things moving dangerously fast, or halting suddenly to listen for what might be ahead or behind, as when a driver ends "staring / Out at the Pole Star through a window of bone". Paranoia and exhaustion infect the gardener's wife, who barricades her front door with thousands of cans of catfood in case of famine, no less than

> a fly's black torso,
> deep in the mire of last year's dust,
> with its seraph wings still poised for flight
> but cumbersome like panes
> of leaded glass or paddles of cracked quartz,
> tired for a while of beating at the air.

McKendrick's linguistic precision unsettles, his hyphenated and compound words heightening the hybrid atmosphere. His poems clatter on pitch with phrases like, "clove-hitch" and "blunt-hulled", "leafmash" and "cotter-pin", "gutstring" and "a lizard canopening a cricket". His purpose is not always to arrest, however, as shown in the prophesying onomatopoeia of this passage from 'A Flight of Locks':

> so water sluices through the culverts
> on either side of the lock's brick chamber
> in swags and scallops and volutes
>
> burled and blurred and bossed and scooped
> like a crystal maelstrom in a bottleneck
> crizzling its uprush in a double ridge
>
> till risen it overrides itself...

His longer lines paradoxically voice the inhale of panic or the exhale of fatigue more successfully than do the truncated lines of 'Taken Awares' or 'The Best of Things', where the brevity of inconclusions like "have a nice day" is lacklustre. Only the final poem, an exchange of monologues by Galatea and Polyphemus, fails by being off-the-cuff; the rest live up to the opening poem's "baleful auguries". Readers seeking emotional urgency or neighbourly compassion will find neither in *The Marble Fly:* its manic attacks and passive resistance evoke a wry unease and dis-ease, with ease.

Quaquaversalities

by James Keery

DICK DAVIS

Touchwood

Anvil, £7.95
ISBN 0 85646 269 1

IAIN BAMFORTH

Open Workings

Carcanet, £7.95
ISBN 1 85754 257 6

TOUCHWOOD CONTAINS TWO admirable poems. 'Comfort' is one of them:

> Insomnia: I get up, read, then write,
> A bit of consciousness alone at night.
> The house is cold; after an hour or two
> I stumble back to darkness, warmth and you.
> You are asleep but as I gingerly
> Edge into bed, you turn to welcome me:
> No comfort I have known in any place
> Can equal that oblivious embrace.

'A Qasideh for Edgar Bowers' is not the other, but it reaffirms Davis's faith in "the poems I / Was all those years ago bowled over by". His 1978 review of *Living Together* is superb criticism, particularly in its comparison with Valéry, but also an exercise in self-regard:

> The title of the book is an immense cold irony – the person with whom the poet lives is himself ... even when one turns to the world it is inevitably the world

conditioned by one's self that one perceives ... the solitude of our condition, the struggles of the mind to know itself and the world mirrored in the self.

In its edginess, abstraction and self-pity, its solipsism, 'Comfort' is the quintessential Davis poem. That "oblivious embrace" is beautiful, but in exalting it above a conscious one, Davis reinforces the mythopoeic implications. "A bit of consciousness alone at night" is symbolic of "the solitude of our condition", from which Lethean oblivion is a comforting release. The myth of Narcissus informs successful lyrics from earlier collections ('Narcissus' Grove'; 'Night on the Long-Distance Coach'; 'Government in Exile'; 'Climbing'), but Davis's finest poem expresses the "immense cold irony" of love by means of a different myth: "Irony is the dead"

> Who are not saved but see
> Magnificent bold Orpheus
> Claim the incredulous
> Soon-to-return Eurydice.

It is "incredulous", perfect as epithet and rhyme, that brings the unrecognising shade of 'Comfort' miraculously to life. As a sceptical evocation of the Orpheus myth, 'Irony and Love' bears comparison with Winters's elegy for Crane.

'Comfort' also illustrates the two-dimensional quality of Davis's language, another of his own traits that the poet-as-reviewer has singled out for praise: "intimately concerned with surfaces... Gunn's poems are definite, precise... They proceed logically ... and work to a conclusion". Hence "that lack of resonance of which some critics have complained". The trouble is that most of the poems in *Touchwood* fall well below the gold-standard. Notably 'Gold':

> Its atavistic glitter will not fade
> And that's the point: barbaric power and pride
> (Piled torques and rhytons gaudy in a grave)
> Point to the presence of what lived and died.

What is a reader supposed to do with such inert, self-satisfied, not even well-crafted musings, reminiscent of the worst excesses of Movement moderation? Can't we have a first line that makes its *own* point? And look at those trivially alliterative pairs. Davis actually imputes to a barbarian chieftain the dying wish "To lodge a fragment in eternity". Does

he think rhytons were *intended* to fragment? The poem fails to justify its complacent QED.

Not that 'Gold' is the worst poem in the book. My nominations would include 'A Monorhyme for Miscegenation', which extols marriages such as the poet's own ("Black / White, Jew / Gentile, Moslem / Me"), in which "all desired and decent virtues" are made manifest. Davis *might* have got away with this if it weren't for 'After the Angels', just over the page: "The pretty mandarin ducks / That pair off once, for life" – so much for miscegenation!

The poem that really did it for me, though, is 'We Should be so Lucky': "Here is a shameful, strong / Nostalgia – to have been / A minor functionary / At some resplendent scene" . For Davis *is* a "minor functionary" – Professor of Persian at Ohio State University – and late-twentieth-century America a scene of such barbaric splendour as to make a medieval Persian court turn pale. The combination of fawning on the famous ("glad to be your pupil / In this, if a lollygagging, laggard / One, now verse is my bag" – 'In Praise of Auden') and contempt for the "lumpen mob" of his colleagues ('Tenured in the Humanities') seems suited to the "court panegyrist" Davis wishes he had been.

Thank goodness for 'Into Care':

> Here is a scene from forty years ago:
> A skinny, snivelling child of three or so
>
> Sits on a table, naked and shamefaced.
> A woman dabs his body to the waist
>
> With yellow pungent ointment and he feels
> Her shock as she remarks, "Look at the weals
>
> On this boy's back." Her colleague steps across:
> Gently she touches him. He's at a loss
>
> To think what kind of "wheels" she sees, but knows
> That here at least there will be no more blows.

Is the child Davis? Date and age check out (born 1945; *Touchwood* collects poems from 1988). Yet there is nothing coy about the detachment from that "skinny, snivelling child", rather a chillingly persistent, irrational sense of shame. The poem is clinical yet "intimately concerned with surfaces", as in the transmission through the child's skin of the nurse's shock. Can 'We Should Be so Lucky' be the work of the same poet? The world is strange.

Iain Bamforth

Movement in Davis's poetry is almost invariably a vector through two-dimensional space, whether physical or conceptual. By contrast, Iain Bamforth takes as his epigraph an axiom from Lobachevski: "The shortest distance between two points is not always a straight line". We may expect to find ourselves in non-Euclidean space, in which a "near-Gaussian distribution of observation points" occasions "hypertrophic exuberance":

> Quaquaversalities, cornycracks of the metamidi,
> Scotch reviewers'
> scotomata, gallusrictus, readywise-readmes,
> melimelos, sans-
> caniculottes, Desperantists, scotologicologophobists...

'Impediments' is a Joycean sequence of Parisian "autographemes" which makes constant reference to Bamforth's native Scotland and to his métier as a GP. It's a pleasure to puzzle out the "pizzled quotatoes", and often worthwhile: "scotomata", or blind-spots, is a shrewd dig at Byron's "Scotch Reviewers"; and I like "scotologicologophobists", too, in exchange for which I offer Bamforth a "scotograph", or "machine for writing in darkness" ("scoto-": comb. form of Gk *skotos* darkness") – resisting temptation to ask if he already has one!

For oblique Bamforth may be, but not obscure. *Sophistication* is the keynote of *Open Workings,* from the cover inwards. 'An die Schönheit' (1922) by Otto Dix depicts contemporary figures in a dark ballroom and, on the skin of a bass drum, a deficient-looking Indian chief, whose headdress mirrors that of one of the women; another is clad only in corsetry, while a third is meretriciously made-up. All shrink beside the harshly-lit, ashen-faced, immaculate pugnacity of the central male, who regards the spectator through narrowed eyes, one hand strangling a telephone. A misogynistic allegory, the painting seems to me, for all its brilliance and black humour, an unfortunate choice; give or take a few smart phrases – "perfunctory double-backings of the beast" – there is nothing so unpleasant inside the book. Or perhaps it's a joke, and the baleful protagonist (Dix himself) is a doctor on call? If so, I think it's funny, but the doubt crystallises my anxiety about the poetry, so enthusiastically hypersophisticated as to verge on the naive.

Naivety takes the form of emulation, not least of Muldoon – "nothing goes, except without saying";

"Justice, she shyly insisted, was just ice" – but chiefly of the pulchritude of Mr Ashbery:

> And the reasons were always bog-eyed, amazed at the
> world's analysis
> of its own problems, rainy curtains and the light
> frotted gold,
> and mine of their digitalised fluttering bird-hearts,
> stroked by my hand
> as if to confirm them language was only ever a slow
> fugue.

Syntax is the minimum pleasure of reading Ashbery, even at low pressure; but the clumsiness and solecism of that last line are uncharacteristic of Bamforth, who skilfully adapts the expansive style to the rigours of his ethnographic landscapes: "Some winters, though, there'd be utter stillness, and a fogbound / grievousness ...";

> Somehow, it's the remembered life: as if we had
> blown here like
> itinerant potato-pickers with the August winds,
> sipping peatish rain
> as it slowly turns to whisky in a cooper's sump.

Like many Scottish poets, from MacDiarmid, Graham and Singer to Frank Kuppner, Bamforth needs elbow-room. 'Doing Calls on the Old Portpatrick Road' has its disquieting moments – "I was there to give bad news / and watch what they'd do with it" – and its parodic ones – "a neuk then, sleeved with its bellibuchts" – but among its 30 sections is 'On Airyhemming Farm':

> Once, penning the sheep,
> she'd been struck by lightning. It sparked
> sixty more years, till the rasp
> of chronic illness. A cautionary tale,
>
> but who would have stinted her that one exalting
> moment on a hammock of turf –
> to have seen a bucket fly and to get up herself,
> black as sin, next to her charred sheep ...

The Scottish combination of pitiless wit – lightning as a kind of cosmic ECT; the ground suddenly as precarious as a "hammock"; the anti-parabolic "charred sheep" – and admiring compassion finds perfect, if ironic, expression in the Old English of "sparked", "rasp" and "stinted". I must admit that this poet is growing on me at an alarming rate.

JENNY JOSEPH
CALLING SHIPS AT SEA

There are several ways of calling ships at sea, the telephone directory tells us.

Instead of area codes there are ocean codes (a slip of the finger on the dial and you'd get the Pacific instead of the Atlantic Ocean [east]). You'd need of course to know the ship's name and give the name of the radio station, if known. (How one could give it if not known I'm not sure but then I sometimes find the simplest instructions baffling if you read them carefully).

If your ship has satellite communications you can even dial direct if the exchange you're dialling from has digital metering. Imagine dialling and hearing it ringing, ringing in all that waste of waters, the dark wave blotting out the cloud-covered sky for hundreds and hundreds of miles and the shrill of the telephone, a muffled trilling in a cupboard among floating spars. Of course you'd need to know the identification number of this ship all at sea that you are wanting to call.

There is even a way of finding out its region code if you don't know it, but for that to be of much use I suppose one would need to know which ocean the ship, listing dangerously, its ballast shifted, fuel tank holed, low down in the water out of control before the storm, was in. Looking under Inmarsat will tell you the ocean code (Atlantic Ocean, west – 874, Indian Ocean – 873, Pacific – 872) but not the ocean, not warn you of that great mass of water filling the horizon, its currents, its rocks, its furies.

Oh ship all at sea, engine fouled, broken-backed, the long rollers running from the horizon pouring through your hold on their remorseless momentum across the world, if I had, never mind what equipment, it is as unlikely you would hear me as when I stand on a cliff and call into the wind. And if you heard, what could that do for you, driven to jagged straits by the inexorable South-Easter, into the suck, strong as death, of the coiling currents?

> To direct dial your Inmarsat calls:
> 010
> followed by Ocean region code
> followed by ship's identification no.

Yet I climb to the cliff-top and I call. Who knows but that somewhere in the shriek of the storm sawing through the steel hawser, in some vibration from the ocean's pounding you may imagine you hear the tones of a voice?

From *Extended Similes*, published by Bloodaxe in June.

Canon Fodder

by Tim Kendall

The Norton Anthology of Poetry
4th edition

Eds. Margaret Ferguson, Mary Jo Salter,
Jon Stallworthy
Norton, £17.95
ISBN 0 393 96820 0

DANTE, IT IS often said, was the last writer to assimilate the sum of available human knowledge. By necessity we are all specialists now. How many poets, for example, are capable of saying anything sensible about string theory, or even, for that matter, about *La vita nuova*? This increasing fragmentation of knowledge has ushered in the age of the anthology, a genre much derided because it emphasises the superficiality of our expertise. We may not have time to listen to Puccini, but would never dare admit to relying on the Three Tenors to pick out the "best" bits for us.

If my experience of anthologies is typical, most of us will immediately look up our personal obsessions and hobby-horses, then feel irritated when we see that our favourite writers are unrepresented, understocked, or represented by unimaginative selections. Turning to William Dunbar's poetry in the latest edition of the *Norton Anthology*, for example, I find he is given just two poems: the already-familiar 'Timor Mortis Conturbat Me'; and the worthy but pedestrian 'In Prais of Wemen', which has replaced, from the third edition, the clamorous magnificence of 'Done is a Battle'. The suspicion must be that the inclusion of such relatively dull work has been motivated by extra-poetical criteria – a suspicion reinforced by the fact that the blurb, the press release and the anthology's preface all over-insistently stress the number of female poets represented. Ironically, the acceptable message of 'In Prais of Wemen' is subverted by an editorial error. The poem contains the lines,

> Rycht grit dishonour upoun him self he takkis
> In word or deid quha evir women lakkis;

By glossing "lakkis" erroneously, as "likes" rather than "disparages", the editors inadvertently destroy the agenda proclaimed by the poem's title.

Perhaps a volume of this immensity – 2000 pages, at under a penny a page – should be allowed the occasional slip. But the *Norton Anthology* has long since won the right to be judged by the highest standards. Its shortcomings are mostly the result of misdirected good intentions: although the editors have thought of everything, sometimes their conclusions are questionable. The treatment of Wyatt's 'They Flee from Me' is a revealing example. The third edition printed a compromise between rival manuscript versions. Acknowledging textual complications, the fourth publishes both the Egerton and the Tottel, giving them equal credence, even though the former was copied by Wyatt himself, while the latter seems to have been cack-handedly "corrected" after the poet's death to suit Tottel's cloth ear. Unlike the two versions of Dickinson's 'Safe in their Alabaster Chambers–', which the *Norton Anthology* usefully publishes together, this is an instance where completeness should have given way to editorial discernment. And if the editors are intent on being fastidious, they ought to transcribe more closely: the Egerton manuscript reads (with spellings modernised) "Therewithal sweetly did me kiss", not "And therewithal...".

'They Flee from Me' also highlights the dangers of explanatory notes. When Wyatt's persona, complaining that women now avoid him, remembers that "Thanked be fortune, it hath been otherwise / Twenty times better", the footnote mysteriously reads "i.e., more than twenty times". This does nothing to interpret the boastful *double entendre*: "Twenty times better" could mean either very much better, or better on twenty separate occasions. Wyatt's ambiguities evade the editors again later, as the lover complains of his abandonment:

> But since that I so kindely am served,
> I would fain know what she hath deserved.

It is unclear why the spelling of "kindely" alone remains unmodernised. However, the editors do help elucidate the word's subtleties, rightly pointing out that its usage is at once ironic (the lover has not been treated kindly) and bitter (female "kind" always treats men this way). To stop the analysis at this point is to turn 'They Flee from Me' into a sulky and self-pitying gripe. In fact "kindely" also incriminates the male speaker: he is treated according to his kind, meaning either that nice guys like him always get messed around, or, by contrast, that he is being paid back "in kind" – getting a dose of his own medicine. By unpacking some meanings at the expense of others, the Norton editors simplify Wyatt's multilayered genius.

It is a shame that these details should detract attention from the ambition of the Norton enterprise. The anthology's first edition appeared in 1970, and its three subsequent incarnations provide an invaluable education into the ways canons are formed and reformed as fashions change. Certain writers, Dunbar included, seem to be looked on with disfavour: no Lydgate, Gower or Henryson (all, surely, major medieval poets), no Oldham, no W. S. Graham, and among living poets no Stephen Dobyns or Christopher Reid. Devotees need not despair just yet; quoting M. H. Abrams, the preface to the fourth edition notes that "a vital literary culture is always on the move". The appearance of Clough's poetry after a prolonged and inexplicable absence is one of forty examples of pre-twentieth-century poets being allowed past the bouncers for the first time. Nevertheless, the redress has been only partial: an anthology of this size ought to find room, if not for the whole of Clough's *Amours de Voyage*, then at least for considerably more than the first three letters.

Of course, such whingeing is a favourite sport among reviewers, who complain about the editors' exclusions without considering that the space created for each new poet will result in losses elsewhere. The ejection of Browning's 'Caliban upon Setebos', for example, helps make room for the modest selection of Clough's poetry. The obvious way the *Norton Anthology* can (and, undoubtedly, should) provide us with both the Browning and the Clough is to rectify its curious prejudice towards the twentieth century. Julia Ward Howe, who died in 1910, appears almost half-way through the book; and Basil Bunting, the first represented poet born in our century, occurs seven hundred pages before the end. Only the most incorrigibly delinquent of critics would argue that over one-third of the greatest English-language poetry has been written by poets born between 1900 and 1960. Presumably the Norton editors are responding to the pressures of the market-place, but when the Gawain-poet is assigned three pages and E. E. Cummings eight, we know perspectives have become skewed.

Admittedly, the twentieth century poses peculiar problems for the anthologist. We may squabble over whether or not obviously minor poets like Isaac Watts should be included, but everyone (or at least, everyone worth listening to) would expect to see Swift and Pope. Where post-war poets are concerned there is as yet no such consensus. The Norton policy is to avoid offence by including a sprinkling of poems by just about everyone, in line with Yeats's famous proclamation to the Rhymers' Club in the early 1890s: "None of us can say who will succeed, or even who has or has not talent. The only thing certain about us is that we are too many". This is pure diplomacy, perhaps we cannot "say", but the perceptive among us will, hopefully, be right more often than not. It would have been preferable had the anthology adopted a more adventurous approach, by halving the number of twentieth-century poets – who are considerably "too many" – and increasing the remainder's selection. If the editors want to pursue their generous attitude toward modern writers, they might consider publishing separate volumes for pre- and post 1900 poetry, and stressing that different selection criteria are being employed in each. At the moment the anthology is in danger of being seen to promote a tacit and fatuous belief in literary progress: the later the period, the richer the harvest .

These flaws are conspicuous because they stand out from what is otherwise an extraordinarily impressive design. Too many anthologies feel like they could easily have been thrown together in half an hour down the pub, with editors scrawling the titles of their favourite poems on the backs of beer mats. The *Norton Anthology* is an altogether different kind of enterprise, much more purposeful and serious-minded, yet without pedantry. It is easy to see why the anthology should have become an essential teaching aid in schools and university departments throughout the world. As a pedagogic tool it easily outperforms its rivals. A new and welcome feature in this fourth edition is the opening up of intertextual "dialogues" between poems and poets, highlighted by cross-referencing annotations: never again will tutors need to sit up all night devising Practical Criticism papers. But the pleasures and usefulness of this book allow it to appeal far beyond the academy. Both the sensible (presumably co-authored) preface and Jon Stallworthy's excellent introductory essay on versification immediately reassure us we can trust the editors to lead us safely through the highways and byways of English-language poetry. This is still the anthology to keep on the bookshelf beside your Complete Shakespeare and King James Bible.

That's How It Was

by William Scammell

JAMES KNOWLSON

Damned to Fame: The Life of Samuel Beckett

Bloomsbury, £25
ISBN 07475 2719 9

I'M ALWAYS PLEASED to meet the late risers among us. Byron didn't get up till noon. Cyril Connolly rocked in bed moaning "poor Cyril!". Robert Frost's cows had to wait an unconscionable time before being let out to pasture. Beckett seldom saw daylight until Sol was halfway across the heavens and speeding breakneck for the edge of the world.

* * * * *

"Let me cry out then, it's said to be good for you". "Not to want to say, not to know what you want to say, not to be able to say what you think you want to say, and never to stop saying, or hardly ever, that is the thing to keep in mind, even in the heat of composition".
"There is no use indicting words, they are no shoddier than what they peddle".

* * * * *

Every so often during this epic read of 850 pages I got so parched I had to stop and dip into the well of Beckett's own prose, which is essentially poetry by other means, which in turn explains why poets have long regarded him as one of their own. The stories and novels tell you everything you'll ever need to know about his "themes", dreams and obsessions, hence what's going on in all that lessness on stage and page. Every sentence is stripped and given a physical to ensure that it's fit to bear the burden of Beckett's nimble and remorseless mind. It reminds me, in this respect, of the weight and balance of an Isaac Babel sentence in Babel's short stories, and of passages in Jean Rhys and Scott Fitzgerald – what oft was thought but seldom driven so well past the hapless goalie of culture.

* * * * *

Poetic prose is a bit of a strange animal in English, as opposed to, say, Russian or Spanish, where there is a tradition in these things. You can see it going wrong in Lawrence Durrell, Djuna Barnes, Gertrude Stein, parts of Malcolm Lowry and Woolf, the Stephen Dedalus side of the young Joyce, Nabokov and Updike – too self-conscious and gemlike by half, the mind congratulating itself on its own footwork. A Martin Amis sentence is a species of performance poetry, always keen to raise a laugh. Julian Barnes' prose is more flexible, less defensive, but with a tendency to bow down before the altar of Art. Neither has the courage or range of a Bellow or Rushdie, whose idioms seem able to embrace everything under the sun.

Poetry can learn from prose, as Pound said long ago. John Ashbery and Frank O'Hara were listening. See Ted Hughes's *Moortown* sequence for further developments. See Weldon Kees and Charles Simic. See Michael Hofmann, Muldoon, Selima Hill, Kathleen Jamie, Jamie McKendrick. And see where it turns leaden in the more world-weary bits of the recent Faber anthology *Emergency Kit*, when manner tries to substitute for matter – the Wallace Stevens syndrome, only nowadays it's a longing for life over art and sermons in the very humblest parts of speech.

* * * * *

Knowlson has done a solid, decent, scholarly job of work, unadorned by the proxy "creativity" of a Richard Holmes or Peter Ackroyd. It doesn't soar, neither does it fell you like an ox, as Mrs Gaskell's *Charlotte Brontë* does. He corrects Deirdre Bair's pioneering biography at various points, and adds a good deal to what is known about the Beckett story, but he has almost nothing of Bair's verve and readability. He's an expert on the plays and their staging, and devotes a great deal of space to their genesis, sources, and rehearsal. Beckett's connoisseurship in music and painting is brought out as never before. On the novels he's decent but perfunctory.

* * * * *

And the life itself? Heroic, but with the usual human admixtures. Born Good Friday, exclamation mark, 1906. Middle-class Irish protestant family. Loved his uncomplicated father, loved–hated, for most of a long lifetime, his difficult mother. Brilliant student but ran away from academic career to Paris and the modernists, remaining though as rooted in childhood memories as his heroes Proust and Joyce. Knew the *Divine Comedy* by heart, no figure of speech intended. Publicly sardonic and shy about love and sex but knotted up a string of girlfriends, mistresses, confidantes (in a dozen countries) as long and as tricky as a tennis player's arm. Nobody worked harder or lived poorer. When he had money – and he became a very rich man – he gave much off it away, though not quite all, like Wittgenstein. The pimp who stabbed him in Paris, for no reason, got two months. And apologised. Worked in the Resistance, escaping arrest by a hair's breadth. Later was implacable towards all tyrannies, especially the Stalinist ones and the Irish censors.

* * * * *

"Drowned in dreams and burning to be gone".
"Take on a little contour, for the love of God".

* * * * *

Doctor Johnson was another hero. He meditated a play about him and Mrs Thrale; later, one simply about Johnson and his cat Hodge. Johnson's terror spoke to his own terror. "All poetry is prayer", said Beckett, when he was still saying things. He denied stoutly that his famous absentee character had anything to do with God. How fortunate then, or unfortunate, or undecidable, that his name just happened to remind ear and eye of the Almighty.

* * * * *

The loner had multitudes of friends, chiefly painters, composers, actors, "poets", layabouts, rogues; not many writers, and those mainly lesser fry. "A modern Diogenes", said the Latin orator when Beckett was awarded an honorary degree by his old college, Trinity. Sam said nowt, secure in the tub of his mind. "He is gentle, arrogant, not wanting to discuss but to assert", said Peter Hall. Dennis Potter waxed indignant in his TV column in the *Sunday Times*. Where was Beckett's humanity? Pinter, Havel, Ionescu, Giacometti and dozens more recognised the real thing when they saw it, and took notes.

* * * * *

"There in the sunken head the sunken head".
"Names gone and when to when".

* * * * *

The later years were a whirl of theatres and honours, of deaths and more female friendships, of withdrawals in order to write. Suzanne, his long-suffering mistress, wife and helpmeet, was evidently as difficult and as indispensable as his own right arm. "You are not one of those who give themselves away in small change", said Havel gratefully when Beckett wrote *Catastrophe* for him. Nosirrr.

"Damned to fame" is a *mot* from Pope's *Dunciad*. Will it do, though? There's always anonymity and silence.

DAVID MOORCROFT
P. S.

I met a tradesman from an antique store
Who said: "Two legless nymphs in alabaster
Lie smashed outside the door; some Grecian shards,
Platonic fragments, clutter up the floor.
High on the gaping wall in well-hung plaster
A limping bust of His Lordship looks askew
At a drained magnum of 'Blithe Spirit', eight
Per cent, D.O.C., propped up by the grate.
A word-weary skylark twitters up the flue.
Over the desk, beside an unstrung lyre,
In Gothick lettering these words declare:
'My name is Perse the Peacock, king of bards –
'Lock up your pens, ye poets, and retire!'
A breathless gust of west-wind stirs the sheaves
Of unacknowledged legislation, heaves
A sigh about the room and up the stair,
Puffs out the shattered lamp before its flight
Is spent upon the silence of the night."

Public Poet

by Stephen Burt

Tony Harrison: Loiner

Edited by Sandie Byrne
Oxford University Press, £25
ISBN 019 8184 30 1

TONY HARRISON IS 60 this year, and this may be one of his birthday presents: it opens with a new sonnet of his, ends with verse by Bernard O'Donoghue and Desmond Graham, and fills the 200 pages between with memoirs and admiring essays. Byrne's introduction details Harrison's publishing history, along with the public roles and attitudes Harrison has taken. Graham's essay recalls the University of Leeds in 1959–60, when he, Harrison, Jon Silkin and Geoffrey Hill (!) shared audience and airspace: Graham also lauds (and reprints) an uncollected poem from 1961. Richard Eyre says, mostly, how much he likes working with Harrison; Melvyn Bragg describes at length Eyre's famous video for v.

Then the explications start. Byrne studies Harrison's allusions, concluding that Harrison is not much like Donne, but more like Marvell, and that Gray's Elegy is conservative, orderly, and stately, as Harrison's v. mostly isn't. N. S. Thompson says Harrison's "high art is used against itself; it is used against the holders of culture", and that Harrison is a lot like Donne, since both poets spin public and violent concerns off against private sexual ones. Jem Poster says Harrison's "tacit insistence on the value of formal containment is qualified by repeated acts of subversion, by a series of controlled assaults on his own skilfully fashioned structures", which is at least as true of Heaney, Herbert, Hopkins, H.D. and Hill. Christopher Butler, in the best of the academic contributions, argues that Harrison asks us to imagine, not just competing "cultures" (aitchless v. R.P., women v. men) but also conflicting definitions of "culture" — as privileged, inherited art works, say, versus as a whole way of life. Butler sees such conflicts in The Trackers of Oxyrhynchus, in the flap over Eyre's video, and in v. itself, whose "whole strategy... is to 'give some higher meaning to'" the skinhead's challenge "by provoking an interpretation of it". Harrison ends up (1) a liberal and (2) a comic poet:

his speedy metaphors, fluent puns and dramatic postures "open up the room for manoeuvre between positions". (Butler also notes the "working-class myth" which cannot help informing the sonnets.)

Rick Rylance finds the worries of the late-Cold War Left not just in the play about Greenham Common and the poems about nuclear apocalypse, but in the sonnets about World War II and in Harrison's Oresteia. Martyn Crucefix on 'Metre and Voice in the Poems' concludes, roughly, that the poems he likes most contain more than one of each. The classicist Oliver Taplin tracks the female choruses in Harrison's dramatic works: Harrison "has been a step ahead of the vanguard of classical scholarship" both in placing the chorus at the centre of performance and in making us think about its gender. He also, usefully, describes a few works as produced, confirming my impression that the teleplay The Big H must have been even funnier, and more moving, on screen than on the page.

Most essays sound desperate to link Harrison to the highest of high-culture pedigrees, however much they say he calls their privilege into question: we hear of Metaphysicals, the Lyrical Ballads, and of course the Greeks, but not of Dryden, late-'thirties Auden, Shelley's Swellfoot the Tyrant, The Beggar's Opera, or Elvis Costello. I blushed to find my take on the nondramatic verse shared only by the editor of this journal, Peter Forbes, who explains that Harrison started out in thrall to early Robert Lowell (yes) and then, powered by Greek and Latin, took a flying leap backward over Romanticism and Modernism, coming to rest in eighteenth-century doctrines, half Pope and half Gray (not by the way, Burke's) according to which verse should be a fluent, entertaining exposition of ideas and sensations the reading public already knows. This "working-class neo-Augustanism" fits "Harrison's belief that poetry should appear in newspapers, onstage and wherever the culture is vibrant", and allows him to sound passionate and aggressive within familiar forms – he is never, Forbes says, pedestrian, because his subjects so often smack us in the face: Alzheimer's disease, Armageddon, graveyard-descrecrating yobs, the Gulf War. This account of his style explains how I can enjoy and remember the less personal sonnets and most of v., without minding the clichés or missing the introspection – and how the classicist who once wrote dramatic monologues about syphilis became (like the Kipling who wrote 'Recessional') "a cause celèbre" by means of "a poem you could understand".

IN APPRECIATION OF

Allen Ginsberg 1926–1997

by Adrian Mitchell

WHENEVER I SAW him, I always made my way through the crowd and hugged him. We'd swap a few words and then I'd fade away. Allen had already given me plenty, and there were always hundreds of others who needed his words, his warmth and sometimes his blood. It often seemed he would be eaten alive by his admirers.

Cancer took my mother and my father. Now it has taken Allen, the great-grandson of William Blake, grandson of Walt Whitman, son of William Carlos Williams.

My first meeting with Allen Ginsberg. It was the morning of January lst,1964, a snowy morning and the whole city hung over – a hell of a time for me to give my first poetry reading at a New York coffee-house.

There were about nine people in the audience – my wife and two English friends – and Allen with his partner Peter Orlovsky. After a nervous reading of the mostly conventional poems I wrote at the time, Allen talked to me.

Kindly he picked on the one poem which he really liked – an unfinished, rough draft of an elegy for my mother. "This is the one", he said. "Why don't you write more like that? It sounds like you talking. Listen to the rhythms of your own voice and try to use those rhythms" – and so on.

Now most poets who offer advice to a poet should be ignored, because they want you to be just like them, only not quite so good. But Allen wanted me to be me – and his advice certainly helped to

change the course of my poetry and my life.

The Roundhouse in the mid-sixties. A couple of thousand of us packed into seats in a steamy arena. Allen greeted us by walking round and round the outside of the crowd, clinking his little handbells and chanting.

The first time he circled us there were quite a few giggles – the English embarrassed by simplicity. The second time he circled us the chanting was working, calming our minds. He circled us a third time and our hearts were with him.

In the first half of the evening he performed poems by William Blake, in the second half, his own poems. His performance was full of music, and magic and wonder.

In between poems he talked to us. You felt as if he was talking directly to you. He explained that he used to be full of fear – fear of disease, fear of mockery, fear of being beaten up, fear of police etc. So he made a list of all those fears, small and large. Then he worked through his list, ridding himself of one fear after another and ticking them off on the Fear List.

"And now", he said, "I don't think there's anything I'm afraid of". And you knew it was true, and you knew that you were in the good company of one of the bravest people on the planet. Me, I went home and wrote a list of my Top Twenty Fears. I've got it down to fourteen now.

Allen has been consistently undervalued by

tight-arsed English poetry reviewers, who have reacted like opera buffs exposed to Bessie Smith. He didn't need reviewers.

Although he was one of the greatest performers of this century, he was too dangerous and unpredictable for television. TV's loss.

He had the enthusiasm and love of audiences all over the world. Of course *Howl* and *Kaddish* are now established classics. But many of the later poems will also last for ever.

He didn't much want to write about politics, but how could he help it? He had to be active – in demonstrations against the Vietnam War, racism, nuclear war, gay repression, Allen was there, marching, writing and organizing.

He wasn't politically naive. When you read the transcripts of public discussions with 'sixties gurus like Benjamin Spock or Timothy Leary, it is nearly always Allen who asks the practical down-to earth questions: How many of our people have been arrested? Where are they? How can we bail them?

What do we do next?

He made trouble of the highest quality, whether by chanting in a Chicago courtroom or confessing to wet dreams about Che Guevara in Havana. Or simply by performing honest poems.

There are many Americas. Eisenhower and Kennedy spoke for one of them. Martin Luther King Junior spoke for another.

But Allen was the most articulate prophet of the New Bohemian revolution, an international movement which believes the arts can change the world – for better or worse. He was our poet and our prophet and we loved him.

After I heard of Allen's death on the radio, I rang up Brian Patten to tell him the news and we shared our grief for our disreputable older brother. I tried to tell Brian what Allen had done for me. All I could manage was: "He set me on fire".

This article first appeared in the *New Statesman* and is reprinted by kind permission.

Tom Rawling 1916–1996

by Anne Stevenson

SLIPPERY FISH AND good poems are alike; and like love, how elusive of the pursuer! Tom Rawling's 'The Names of the Sea-Trout' recites spells for the catch:

The silver one, the shimmering maiden,
The milkwhite-throated bride,
The treasure-bringer from the sea,
Leaper of weirs, hurdler to the hills,
The returning native, egg-carrier,
The buxom lass, the wary one,
The filly that shies from a moving shadow,
The darter-away, the restless shiner...
The strong wench, the cartwheeler,
The curve of the world...

Does a finer fisherman's poem exist? In November 1976, when I first met Tom Rawling at an open poetry session at the Old Fire Station in Oxford, he was famous but not for writing poetry. Although

none of us at the Old Fire Station knew who he was, Ted Hughes would have recognized his name as a knowledgeable contributor to *Trout and Salmon*. In his native Cumberland, where he fished with the late Hugh Falkus, Tom's annual visit was a celebrated event. His Oxford friends knew him as an expert naturalist and gardener, though teaching was the profession to which Tom devoted his manifold talents once he was free of the war. From his youth a radical idealist, Tom chose to teach "ordinary" and later handicapped children for the same compassionate reasons that led him to poetry. He was a natural humanitarian, and in consequence, a sworn enemy to class privilege, bureaucracy and establishment cant.

The son of a war-scarred (and periodically violent) village school-master, Tom rebelled against his North-country parents and, as a young man, headed south to study History at University College, London. He took a postgraduate teaching degree at Goldsmith's and by the autumn of 1939 had found a job in Oxford. There he met his future wife, Eva, also a teacher. They hastily married in March of 1940, a month before Tom was called up for the army. Tom's daughter, Sue, tells me Tom's mother was so horrified at his marrying that she took to her bed for a week. The marriage, though, was a strong one, lasting for over fifty-one years until 1992, when Tom and their two grown-up daughters lost Eva to cancer. After Eva died, Tom wrote three beautiful poems in her memory and then ceased to write poetry altogether.

Tom Rawling served as a gunner during the war, as his recently published 'Gas Drill' attests (see the *Faber Book of War Poetry*, edited by Kenneth Baker) but most of his poems are set in Ennerdale, Cumberland, where members of the Rawling family have been hill-farmers for centuries. As anyone knows who has looked into *Ghosts at my Back* (Oxford, 1982), *The Old Showfield* (Taxus, 1984) or *The Names of the Sea-Trout* (Littlewood Arc, 1993), Rawling's poems, when not centered on fishing, chiefly look back to and celebrate a way of life he associated with his grandparents. In poems like 'Rootcutter', 'The Barn' and most famously, 'Privy', Rawling achieves that exact balance between unsentimental memory and loving reverence that distinguishes the poems of Seamus Heaney. Tom, in fact, dedicated two poems to Heaney, though he wrote, always, out of his own experience. In 'Rootcutter', a piece of "scrap-iron among nettles" brings back "frozen-fingered mornings" when "you had to heave / to start the wheel / ... While stirks stood / Winter prisoners on dung platforms / Bellowing their demands". The final lines are especially remarkable, reaching beyond private memory to "The contract made with beasts we cage, / All a man undertakes / When he leads out the bull".

In 'Privy', shortlisted for the Arvon prize in 1985, animal excretion is seen wonderfully as the bond between man and beast; the poem revels in and reveals the power of words that in Rawling's childhood would have been forbidden him, reserved for "unmentionabale thoughts":

Warm reek of sweat wraps around me, acrid
sweat of work, the tang of harness that has drunk it...
I step back quickly from the spray when a column of
                                          piss
cascades to the cobbles...a white-flecked spate down
                                     the runnel.

Ammonia. Skin around my
nose prickles.
Another back arches, a tail
cocks up, legs straddle
to break wind, then all the
body, bent bow, squeezes
                    out shit.

Tom Rawling first found himself writing poetry when he was teaching handicapped children at the Ormerod School in Oxford. After his retirement in 1977, he was for some reason able to crack open the memory box of his Ennerdale childhood and poems poured forth in floods. We who were his friends in Oxford at the time remember his amazed excitement, his vociferous, Don Quixote-like presence at the Old Fire Station workshop (he later ran it with great effectiveness) together with that vehement, half-modest war cry, "I'm a very *simple* poet, remember. I can only write very *simple* poems". What that meant was, why couldn't we all write poems as clear and as true and as delightful as his.

When I learned of Tom's death in November of last year, I looked out *The Names of the Sea-Trout* he had signed for me in 1993. The poems were as fresh as the occasions they celebrated. All Tom's work is good; some of it is marvellous, but very little – so it seems to me still – qualifies as truly "simple". It is high time a *Collected Poems of Tom Rawling* were available; many hundreds of readers would find it simply irresistible.

IVY GARLITZ

WERD ICH DONNERN HOREN DIE SEE
(after Brecht)

I can hear the sea pounding the rocks.
I can smell the salt when it strikes,
the shit brown sea.
I hear the foghorns
blasting day and night

from the docks.
The cars squeal down the motorway
at the end of the road.
The black bags pile up in the garden next door.
I have to wipe the clothesline

to get rid of the residue from the docks,
the shit brown sea,
that stripes our clothes with tar.
I can hear the sea pounding the rocks
though the shingle beach is miles away.

At night, the clock's red numbers
accuse me, remind me harshly
how much time is left.
The foghorns blow.
I can hear the sea pounding the rocks.

The silence weighs me down like a cloud,
like the spill of gas from the docks:
the police screeched
to stay in, lock the doors and windows.
I can hear the sea pounding the rocks.

It's like in that foreign song,
you left me in silence
because your ship was down at the docks,
quietly – not like our neighbour
shouting "you bastard"

at 3 every morning,
the man who lives with her
slamming the door, racing the engine.
I can hear the sea pounding the rocks,
the shit brown sea.

NEWS/COMMENT

CENTURION TRIUMPHS

We couldn't produce an issue like this without noting that Soamesday duly came and went on June 3rd. Enoch Soames was a fictional writer in Max Beerbohm's 1916 short story of the same name. Soames languished in the 1890s, one of that decade's least sung poets. In 1897 he was overheard by the Devil wishing he could return in a 100 years time to the British Library to consult the vast literature that had by now gathered around his then little noticed books, *Negations* and *Fungoids*. In the story, Soames's wish is granted but he finds only a reference by "T. K. Nupton" noting his appearance in the Beerbohm story. But now we are in the real 1997, the Enoch Soames Society has decided it can do better than fiction. It and the British Library concocted a display of Soamesiana, a critical volume was produced just in time to be logged in the catalogue, the story was broadcast on Radio 4, and at the due time – ten minutes past two – Enoch Soames himself arrived at the Library to inspect his fame. Perhaps it is time for our own *fin de millennium* fictional poet to make his bow?

MAGAZINES REVIVAL

Things had been a bit too quiet on the magazines for for a long time. The best new magazines of the last 10–12 years – *Verse, Rialto, The North* – were all poem-centred. Where were the maverick voices, the dissentient views? Then, in 1995, came *Thumbscrew*. Now well established, it seems to have encouraged a few more. *Metre*, edited by Hugh Maxton, Justin Quinn and David Wheatley is less contentious than *Thumbscrew*, but its roster of poets, including Harry Clifton, James Lasdun, and Gwyneth Lewis, and its determinedly international stance, bode well for the future. *Verse* has changed since Robert Crawford left. Now essentially an American magazine and sometimes running up to 256 pages, it maintains its international flavour and its Scottish link in the form of contributing editor Andrew Zawacki at St Andrews. Then there's *Brangle*, Carol Rumens' magazine from Belfast, which began as a vehicle for Queens' University, but in its second issue features an essay by Michèle Roberts, an interview with Peter McDonald and Medbh McGuckian on men's fiction.

There is a great deal of overlap between the contributors to all these magazines, which suggests that there is a new critical forum coming into being, and there is a very strong Irish connection, *Metre* and *Brangle* coming from there, *Thumbscrew* with strong Irish links. This isn't surprising – criticism has never gone away in Ireland as it has here. Some of the recent delights include David Wheatley on Geoffrey Hill in *Brangle* No 2, Edna Longley on Tom Paulin in *Thumbscrew* No 7, an interview with Peter Porter in *Verse* Vol 13, Nos 2&3, Steve Burt on Muldoon in *Thumbscrew* No 7.

In case this sounds too much like log-rolling (all of these writers often appear in *Poetry Review*), we should point out that *Brangle* 2 has Peter McDonald referring to "the English propaganda press – magazines like *Poetry Review*, whose values are those of the advertising agency and the FR consultancy, and who constantly need to find something 'new' to promote", and that the forthcoming *Thumbscrew*, No 8, has Sheenagh Pugh casting a jaundiced eye on our recent women's issue. As far as we're concerned, these magazines are producing the kind of critical goading without which the culture becomes stagnant.

Brangle, Edited by Carol Rumens, individual copies £3.00 plus 50p p&p from 100A Tunis Road, London W12.

Metre, Edited by David Wheatley, Hugh Maxton, Justin Quinn, Subscriptions Ir £12/stg £15 (3 issues) from *Metre*, Department of English, Trinity College, Dublin.

Thumbscrew, Edited by Tim Kendall, Subscriptions £10 (3 issues) from *Thumbscrew*, PO Box 657, Oxford OX2 6PH.

Verse, Edited by Nancy Schoenberger and Brian Henry, Subscriptions £9 (3 issues) from *Verse*, University of St Andrews, School of English, Fife, KY16 9AL.

MISSING LINKS

In its somewhat ramshackle progress through the mid-20th century, the Poetry Society failed to maintain a complete set of *Poetry Review*. We should be grateful to hear of the existence of copies of the following issues:

Vols 49–53, 1958–1962 – all issues.
Vol 54, no 1, 1963
Vol 62 No 1, 1971
Vol 62 No 3, 1971
Vol 62 No 4, 1971
Vol 65 No 1, 1975
Vol 66 No 1, 1976.

NET VERSE

The recent death of Allen Ginsberg makes this as good a time as any to mention the Literary Kicks site at **http://www.charm.net/~brooklyn/** which has photographs, biographies, bibliographies and lots of other stuff about not only Ginsberg, but Kerouac, Burroughs, and the rest.

If Keats and Shelley are more your cup of tea, then you'll prefer the Keats-Shelley Journal, at **http://www.luc.edu/publications/keats-shelley/ksjweb.htm**. It's really a taster for the paper version, but contains some useful resources and links.

Another taster is for a new, Tasmanian based, arts and literature journal, with a heavy poetry bias, called *siglo*. It looks as if it may well be worth reading; judge for yourself at **http://www.utas.edu.au/docs/siglo**

Anyone who knows Peter Finch's work won't be surprised to learn that he has a web site, nor that it makes imaginative use of the possibilities of the medium. I found his hypertext information page on R.S. Thomas paticularly interesting. Look it up, at **http://dialspace.dial.pipex.com/peter.finch/**

A couple of entertaining, though very different, magazine style sites have popped up recently. *A Little Poetry* at **http://www.geocities.com/SoHo/Lofts/1735/poetryf.html** is worth visiting to experience the fizzing enthusiasm of its owner, Tracee Coleman.

As its name suggests, *The Alsop Review*, at **http://mww.hooked.net/users/jalsop/** is a more sedate e-zine, that wants to be taken seriously, and probably deserves to be. It's well designed, and has a very high standard of poetry. I should warn you that it contains Kirkup's banned poem 'The Love That Dares To Speak Its Name' but don't worry: that page is clearly marked, so you can easily avoid it.

There seems to be some good-natured rivalry about who can produce the longest list of poetry-related sites. Patrick Martin is doing pretty well at the moment, with over 600 links in his Poetry Resource at **http://home.earthlink.net/~pjmartin/**

Tips for good sites are always welcome. Send them to the usual address: **peter@hphoward.demon.co.uk**

THE WHEEL TURNS

The Arts Council have announced their latest round of Writers' Awards, for fiction, poetry, and Literature for Young People. The poets (£7000)

each are Catherine Byron, Maura Dooley, Tony Flynn, Michael Hofmann, and Jo Shapcott. An intriguing name among the fiction awards (also £7000) is that of Charles Osborne, former Literature Director of the Arts Council, the same Charles Osborne who, soon after he left the post, wrote of "my scepticism as to the usefulness, or indeed the propriety, of many of the grants we have made to writers. For a time we were in danger of turning the Arts Council into a literary soup kitchen". He went on to criticise awards his departments had made to established poets: "...why should they receive Bursaries? They will go on writing poems with or without handouts from the public purse". Charles Osborne is not an established novelist, and his award is for an "experimental novel, provisionally titled *Triple Life*". So that's all right then.

COMPETITION

REPORT ON NO 5: COUPLETS FOR CAUSES

No budding Salman Rushdies emerged here. Perhaps advertising jingles are too easy but too hard to do well. Which means that the prize is rolled over for Competition 6.

NO 6: PERSONA GRATA

A new persona can enhance your poetic life, allowing you to tap into areas that your normal poetry self can't reach. Character sketches please for new personas for well-known poets who might need a break from playing being the well-known poet. Deadline: August 20. Up to *six* prime recent books to be won.

LETTERS

CARVED UP

Dear Editor,

One would think that an occurrence of such literary importance as the appearance of Raymond Carver's *All of Us: The Collected Poems* would be worthy of something more than the slipshod treatment given it by Ian Sansom in his review, 'One Big Yawp' (Vol 87 No 1, p55), and certainly one would expect more from a magazine of such calibre as *Poetry Review*.

But maybe it isn't fair to put the blame on Mr. Sansom, as the sentiments expressed in his review may be indicative of a greater problem, namely the huge and seemingly irreconcilable cleft between contemporary American and British poetry.

In terms of genre, short stories and poems are light years apart, despite the many elements that they may have in common (conciseness, compactness, etc.), and there have been few writers who were able to master both. Raymond Carver was one of them. In his poems, the tension of quotidian desperation is as taut as in any of his short stories. The stark realism, the spare treatment, the quiet anguish; they're all there as well, reduced to crystalline, elegant, totally unpretentious compositions that linger in the brain long after having read them.

George Macbeth, writing of Raymond Carver's poetry, referred to it as "The kind of poetry Hemingway might have written". Hemingway did

write poetry, and it was terrible. It seems that he was incapable of distilling the already boiled-down elements of his stories to anything less than the masterpieces that they remain. On the other hand, it was obviously no problem for Hemingway to go overboard in the other direction, as in the tediously overwritten *The Old Man and the Sea*.

Unless Tess Gallagher is keeping something from us, it seems that Raymond Carver's few attempts at longer works remained fruitless. Obviously, Raymond Carver knew what he was best at and, fortunately for the rest of us, he kept at it as long as he could. In his assessment of Raymond Carver's poetry, Mr. Sansom says,

> It is straight-talking, in-your-face writing; there is nothing bogus or worked-up, nothing fake or clever-clever about it; it's down-home, unbuttoned, blue-collar.

Even if I'd never heard of Raymond Carver, this would be reason enough for me to want to read him, and exactly the sort of thing that is so often missing from contemporary British poetry. Not that all poetry should be "folksy" in nature, but so much British poetry these days is so overwrought and pretentious that it borders on the unreadable.

Continuing his assessment, Mr. Sansom says,

> At its best, in the late poems, the poems from the posthumous collection *A New Path to the Waterfall* (1989), it makes one embarrassed at the dilettantism that usually passes for poetry in Britain. But at its worst it often seems shoddy and slap-dash, a product of careless composition...

The dilettantism of British poetry I've already addressed above, and as for the "careless composition" etc... which *Collected Poems* does not contain flaws, inconsistencies, and weak points (I'm thinking of Philip Larkin – that other champion of the colloquial and the quotidian – and all the dross in his *Collected Poems*), and isn't it exactly these inclusions and revelations that make every *Collected Poems* so intriguing and ultimately rewarding?

I certainly hope that Mr. Sansom's review does not deter any potential reader from experiencing some of the best poetry to come out of America in a long time.

Sincerely,
MARK TERRILL
Wacken, Germany

QUOTE MISQUOTE

Dear Peter Forbes,

I enjoyed this Spring's *Poetry Review* (Vol 87 No 1) more than most, perhaps because you side with the social function of poetry. Jenny Joseph's account of the spread of 'Warning' is delightful. She is quite right – to have Mr or Ms Anon steal one's inventions is the ultimate accolade!

But what about misquotes of famous poems? "Fresh fields and pastures new"? or "...go quietly into that good night" (this week's *Radio Times*)? Can readers quote other examples?

Yours sincerely,

SALLY EVANS

Edinburgh

SOME CONTRIBUTORS

Gillian Allnutt's new collection, *Nantucket and the Angel* was published by Bloodaxe in the Spring.

John Burnside's new collection, *A Normal Skin* and his first novel, *The Dumb House*, are published by Cape.

Wayne Burrows was a featured new poet in *PR* Vol 87 No 1.

Stephen Burt is a graduate student at Yale and a regular contributor to *Thumbscrew*.

Harry Clifton's *The Desert Route: Selected Poems* is published by Bloodaxe.

Sarah Corbett won a Gregory this year; her first collection is due from Seren in Autumn 1998.

Martyn Crucefix's third collection, *The Madder Ghost*, is just out from Enitharmon.

Fred D'Aguiar's new collection, *Bill of Rights*, is forthcoming from Chatto.

Michael Donaghy's latest collection is *Errata* (Oxford Poets, 1994).

Helen Dunmore won the 1996 Orange Prize.

Paul Farley won the 1996 Arvon Poetry Competition and was a featured new poet in *PR* Vol 86 No 2.

Ivy Garlitz has been a featured poet in *Thumbscrew*.

Elizabeth Garrett's first collection, *The Rule of Three*, was published by Bloodaxe in 1991.

John Goodby appears in Faber's *Poetry Introduction 8*.

Philip Gross' latest collection is *I. D.* (Faber).

David Hart won the National Poetry Competition in 1995.

Michael Henry's latest collection is *Panto Sphinx* (Enitharmon).

Jane Holland's first collection, *The Brief History of a Disreputable Woman*, is published by Bloodaxe in August.

Matthew Hollis won third prize in the 1996 National Poetry Competition.

Tim Kendall won a Gregory Award this year and is writing a book on Sylvia Plath for Faber.

Hermione Lee's biography of Virginia Woolf was published by Chatto last year.

Gwyneth Lewis's *Parables and Faxes* has just been reprinted by Bloodaxe.

Michael Longley's latest collection is *The Ghost Orchid* (Cape).

Glyn Maxwell was awarded the E. M. Forster Prize this year.

Jayanta Mahapatra is one of India's best known poets; *The Best of Jayanta Mahapatra* was published in India last year.

Ian McMillan was recently appointed Writer-in-Residence at Barnsley Football Club.

Adrian Mitchell's Collected Poems, *Heart on the Left*, is due from Bloodaxe this Autumn.

John Mole's new collection, *For the Moment*, is forthcoming form Peterloo.

Sinéad Morrissey's first collection, *There Was Fire in Vancouver*, was published by Carcanet last year.

Sean O'Brien's long-awaited *The Deregulated Muse* is due from Bloodaxe in July.

Dennis O'Driscoll's new collection, *Quality Time*, was published by Anvil in the Spring.

Maggie O'Farrell is Assistant Arts Editor of *the Independent on Sunday*.

Ruth Padel won the 1996 National Poetry Competition.

Sheenagh Pugh's new collection, *ID'S HOSPIT*, is just out from Seren.

Simon Rae is writing a biography of W. G. Grace.

Lawrence Sail's latest collection is *Building into Air* (Bloodaxe).

Carole Satyamurti's latest collection is *Striking Distance* (Oxford Poets).

Jo Shapcott is co-editor of *Emergency Kit* and the Poetry Society's Writer in Residence on the Internet.

Matthew Sweeney is co-editor of *Emergency Kit*.

George Szirtes's latest collection is *Selected Poems 1976-1996* (Oxford Poets).

Anthony Thwaite's *Selected Poems 1956-1996* is due from Enitharmon in September.

Andrew Zawacki is a contributing editor for *Verse*.